BISMARCK

AND THE

FRENCH NATION

1848–1890

BISMARCK

AND THE

FRENCH NATION

1848–1890

by

Allan Mitchell

Pegasus   New York

A DIVISION OF THE BOBBS-MERRILL COMPANY, INC., PUBLISHERS

For *Catherine* and *Alexandra*

CONTENTS

PREFACE

Many years ago the remarkable British historian G. P. Gooch observed that more was known about the Bismarck era than any other in man's experience. Anyone who has undertaken an investigation of the historical literature of the late nineteenth century can well understand that claim. The archives of Europe literally contain mountains of dispatches, reports, and memoranda. The libraries there and in the United States are crowded with monographs and dissertations. The professional journals provide a steady supplement of argumentation and analysis, theories and statistics. From year to year the sheer volume of publication continues to grow and the pace of research, if anything, seems to quicken. Today infinitely more is known—or is, at least, available to be read—than could possibly have been imagined a generation or two earlier.

Meanwhile, especially during the past decade, many historians have been self-consciously turning a methodological corner. Whereas previous generations of scholars wrestled in the traditional arena of political and diplomatic history with "the Bismarck problem," now their successors have begun to regard that effort with some skepticism and impatience. In the programmatic formulation of a young German historian, Helmut Böhme, an account of Germany's emergence as a great power "can no longer be written as part of Otto von

Bismarck's biography." Hardly less blunt is the statement
of an American colleague, Theodore S. Hamerow, that
"the preoccupation of most scholars with the problems
of statecraft has caused them to neglect the social matrix
of civic activity. . . . We are ready to deal with other
problems." To judge by these and many other similar
pronouncements, the character of historical writing is
now undergoing a profound change.

A full century after the foundation of the Bismarckian Reich we certainly *should* be ready to leave
completely aside such problems as, say, the annexation of
Alsace and Lorraine. But the truth, it seems to me, is that
we are not. There are at least two important reasons why
this is the case. The first has to do, precisely as the critics
have charged, with the extraordinarily conservative
character of the historical profession until very recently.
Reviewing the range of Bismarck studies in preparation
for this volume, I was repeatedly struck by the uniformity of outlook among older historians, even when their
conclusions widely diverged. The flurry of polemical
discussion following the publication of Erich Eyck's
three-volume biography of Bismarck in the 1940's is a
case in point; even those who disagreed with Eyck's an-
swers at least felt that he was putting the right questions.
This suggests to me that the problem lies not so much in
a preoccupation with statecraft as with a too narrow conception of it. To put the issue somewhat baldly, the traditional historian was often satisfied that he had dealt with
social and economic "factors" once he had defined some
politician's grasp of them; he thus tended to equate
politics with the formulation of policy. To this extent
the critics are correct in their diagnosis. But they are,
perhaps, misleading as to the proper cure. What is needed

is not to eliminate biography from history, but to strike a truer balance between them. The insistence on the wonders to be wrought by a straight dosage of economic and social history has a ring of academic self-justification. It would be more accurate as well as more gracious to admit that we still have much to learn about old problems, even by applying the most traditional techniques.

The second reason follows. As historians recast their work in progress or turn their hands to new tasks, they cannot afford to ignore the labor of their predecessors. It is important, after all, to distinguish between the current orientation of research and a comprehensive understanding of the subject. In this case, even if one may assume that speculation about the motivations of any single statesman will henceforth consume far fewer man-hours than in the past, Bismarck will always remain a central point of reference for German history. A recent study by Hans-Ulrich Wehler, while explicitly concentrating on the "objective" circumstances to which Germany's imperial policies necessarily responded, nonetheless takes more than perfunctory note of "Bismarck's penetrating influence." Whatever future controversies may swirl about the character of Germany's economic and social development in the nineteenth century, Bismarck is certain to remain at the eye of the storm. To neglect him would be distorting and self-defeating.

Nothing is to be gained, then, by accepting a false polarity of old-guard and new-wave history. Historians need to continue traditional forms of research and writing, while seeking to improve them; and they need to break new ground both conceptually and methodologically. Writers of history should, in short, be retentive as well as inventive. Since a brief volume such as this cannot hope to perform both functions equally well, an option has generally been made for the former. The reader will find here few eccentric judgments—and none made with the intention of being deliberately outrageous. As a former student of William L. Langer, I am scarcely inclined to the view that little is to be learned from a book simply because it was composed forty years ago. But as the contemporary of many of the authors cited in the bibliography, I have tried to evaluate fairly their contribution and to incorporate their latest findings whenever feasible.

Throughout I have held two objectives in view: to survey the Bismarck scholarship of the past century and to augment it in one specific area where it seems to me insufficient. A recently published bibliography of Bismarckiana lists more than 6000 titles; yet there has been to date no single statement exclusively concerning the special relationship of Bismarck's Germany to France during the entirety of his public career. If a student wished to investigate that problem he was, for lack of a starting-point, confronted either by a bewildering array of monographs or else by a choice among the several broad diplomatic histories and textbooks treating nineteenth-century Europe. My intention has been to prepare for the reader a brief which he can examine from beginning to end at a single sitting, or two, and which he can employ as a tool of orientation. I hope thereby to provide both a concise analysis of the subject and a critical introduction to the pertinent historical literature. This should serve as a guide book which both locates familiar landmarks and points out terrain suitable for further exploration. It is surely unnecessary to stress the inevitable selectivity of this procedure, since my aim has obviously been to write an account which may be useful to students and scholars alike, rather than one which claims to be definitive.

Five friends and colleagues were kind enough to read the manuscript for me: Werner T. Angress, Klemens von Klemperer, Eberhard Kolb, Alain Silvera, and Hans-Ulrich Wehler. Since their reactions and suggestions for revision were quite different, none should feel at all responsible for the final result. But I do want them to know that they each caused me sleepless nights, for which they are hereby forgiven.

A.M.

INTRODUCTION

When the nineteenth century began, France was easily the most dynamic nation on the European mainland. It was the unique combination of a powerful centralized state and the willing allegiance of a talented and energetic populace which made France the natural crucible of European nationalism. The English example, more remote and less volatile, could not have had the same immediate impact. Certainly insofar as the German lands were concerned, at least, the more elemental impulses in the first half of the century came from France.

As incarnated by Napoleon Bonaparte, the French nation represented both a military force and a seditionary threat to the embattled monarchies of central Europe. None of them was left untouched, and many were permanently altered, by the trauma of the French imperium. Yet once Bonaparte was gone, they quickly recovered their equilibrium. It is amazing, in fact, how little remained of the jacobin enthusiasm which had flared sporadically in the two decades before 1815. Whereas French nationalism had taken the form of a crusading mission, the emerging nationalism in Germany was often appropriated by autocratic rulers as an instrument of retrenchment.

This phenomenon was nowhere more apparent than in Prussia. Until the Napoleonic era German nationalism had been a vague, virtually belletristic sentiment of com-

mon language and custom. But thereafter it was clear that
a disembodied national spirit alone could not hope to be
effective in the arena of European power politics. Germany would have to become more like France, a unified
nation-state, or else cease to count. Of course there were
those who wished to continue to give the German nation
the broadest possible definition, thereby including the
German-speaking population of the Habsburg monarchy.
Weighing against such a *grossdeutsch* predilection, however, was the French precedent. There was good reason
to doubt that a loose confederation of German states
could ever hope to attain the strength and coherence required for nationalistic competition. In that case the
German territories would be condemned in the future,
as so often in the past, merely to serve as a battleground
for contesting armies. The logic of this was evident not
only to the Hohenzollern dynasty but also to many German liberals who might otherwise have preferred almost
anything to an extension of Prussian domination in
northern Europe. Still, if nation had to be wedded to
state in order to survive, Prussia was obviously an available candidate—all the more so after the formation of
the Zollverein in the 1830's.

The resolution of this problem is inseparable from
the political biography of Otto von Bismarck. No serious
historian today holds the view of Bismarck as a great
national patriot, possessed from cradle to chancellory of
a master plan to unify Germany, steering a relentless
course toward conflict first with Austria and then—the
culminating Machiavellian act—with France. But neither
is it plausible to adopt an alternative interpretation of his
actions as those of an ordinary politician stumbling
through one diplomatic episode after another in a strictly

fortuitous succession of events. Bismarck was a Prussian nationalist who eventually realized the congruence of dynastic ambitions and German aspirations. To be comprehensible his statesmanship must be observed in a progression of stages, each of which presented timely solutions and posed new problems.

Of critical importance throughout Bismarck's public career was the ubiquitous challenge of the French nation. He was born just as the Bourbon restoration was beginning; and he was already well into his teens when Charles X was turned out by the July monarchy. He grew up among elders who could recall 1789 and who retained vivid memories of Napoleon's armies and the humiliating French occupation of Berlin. The French Revolution was therefore as much a part of his experience as is the Second World War for the present generation of young. This did not mean, needless to insist, that he necessarily adopted the opinions of his seniors, only that the psychic effects of French nationalism were still acute in the consciousness of those from whom he took instruction. From the outset and for the rest of his life, Bismarck was thus forced to cope with France. How he did so is the subject of this book.

I

BEFORE THE CALL
(1848-1862)

Otto von Bismarck's earliest notions of France were conventionally Prussian, a mixture of admiration and distaste. He started learning the French language at the age of eight, later had a Swiss tutor, and apparently became quite fluent even before his university days. One of his first political impressions was at fifteen, when his mother had him read to her aloud from French newspaper accounts of the July revolution in 1830. Yet as a schoolboy he did not share the enthusiasm of some of his classmates for the figure of Napoleon Bonaparte; and later, while a university student at Berlin in 1834, he confessed only half in jest to a "righteous disdain for Jews and Frenchmen."[1] Of his first visit to France, during a trip through the Rhineland in 1837, he later recalled his anger that the

French held Strasbourg and remembered that his emotions became "revengeful and bellicose" at the sight of German territory which had once been invaded by French armies.[2] This scattered evidence is inconclusive, but if one judges a young man by the friends he keeps and the books he reads, Bismarck was more warmly disposed toward England and America. It was not that he grew up with deep and unmalleable prejudices against the French nation; he simply developed no intimate contact with the land beyond the Rhine.

Bismarck was raised as an aristocrat and always thought of himself as such, even though he did not begin to write the "von" before his name until 1848. If he actually held any liberal or republican sympathies as a boy, they were soon submerged by his consciousness of being a Prussian Junker and a faithful adherent of the crown. During his erratic service in the Prussian bureaucracy and in his brief tenure as a delegate to the united diet in Berlin in 1847, he demonstrated his conservatism at every opportunity. He knew little of France at the time and was unpleasantly surprised to learn of the insurrectionary movement there in 1848.[3] Although the first stirrings of revolution occurred in Italy, the decisive signal emanated from Paris in February when the Orleanist monarchy of Louis Philippe was unable to manage crowds in the street. Even for the politically stunted states of central Europe, the proclamation of the Second Republic was an ominous warning of what might happen if radicalism went unchecked. Unlike a half century earlier, Prussia had little immediate reason to fear the incursion of French military forces; the real danger was the now renewed threat of the French precedent.

Bismarck's initial response to the outburst of street-fighting in Berlin in March has often been narrated: his plan to organize a peasant militia force and his efforts to persuade military leaders to strike a decisive counter-revolutionary stroke. Neither proved necessary. Before the year was out Louis Bonaparte had been elected president of the French republic and the situation in Prussia was well in hand. Still a virtually unknown personality in his early thirties, Bismarck played no conspicuous part in the conservative retrenchment which followed in Frederick William IV's abrupt refusal of a crown offered by the Frankfurt parliament.

He was, however, soon afforded an opportunity to participate in the politics of reaction when, in 1851, he was appointed as the Prussian delegate to the resuscitated diet of the German confederation in Frankfurt. It was there that he began to formulate his first coherent views on the French nation. Whatever his preconceptions until then, Bismarck never regarded France as an abstraction thereafter. He was neither a metaphysician nor a man of intractable clichés; his thinking was thoroughly political and therefore closely attuned to real changes in the exercise of power. For that reason the events of 1848 had been significant for him in a way that those of 1851 were not. He professed to be not at all alarmed by Bonaparte's coup d'état on December 2. In Berlin on that day, Bismarck wrote that the news from Paris was received there with "jovial calm" and expressed the opinion that the excited reaction in Frankfurt was neither justified nor desirable. The coup confirmed rather than altered circumstances in France. It was up to the Prussian government to draw the proper conclusions.[4]

After returning to his post in Frankfurt, Bismarck began at once to treat France's transformation from republic to empire as a diplomatic formality. At the same time he was extraordinarily sensitive to questions of protocol and recognized their symptomatic importance. From his garden he could watch the entrance to the residence of the French emissary Tallenay and was thus literally in a position to observe the diplomatic contacts of the smaller German states with France. To Berlin he reported his dismay at the lack of discipline within the German confederation and the inability of its two leading members to exert effective leadership. Although aware that he stood under "suspicion of Bonapartism," he worked for a prompt and unified recognition of Napoleon's regime by all the German courts. His only satisfaction in failing to achieve that objective was that Austria rather than Prussia was generally blamed for the delay, if not for the disunity.[5] In short, Bismarck's primary concern was not with the French form of state as such but with its effect on Prussia's political position in Germany.

In an embryonic version, Bismarck's conception of a sensible Prussian policy was couched in a private letter to the heir apparent, Prince William, in 1853. He reported that a new Austrian minister had recently arrived in Frankfurt with news that Vienna now regarded the international situation with alarm. "It is possible," he wrote— failing to specify whether it was the Austrian view or his own—"that we are closer to war than is assumed in Berlin." Beginning in the Ottoman empire, a conflict might spread quickly to Europe. Rumors were already circulating in the Frankfurt business community of secret preparations by the French army. Even if that were true, it was Bismarck's judgment that Prussia should avoid a precipitous decision to oppose France. Prussia must look to its own interests; and dealing with Napoleon III, rather than with Louis Philippe, at least had the advantage that a realistic assessment of French intentions could be unaffected by "half sympathies" for the July monarchy. If foreign policy were to be guided by political calculation rather than sentiment, there was no immediate reason to assume an "irrevocable and bitterly hostile position toward France," a stance which could only limit Prussia's freedom of action. If war did come, of course, Prussia should not hesitate to join with the other German states in self-defense. But until then it was to Prussia's advantage to behave in such a way "that Russia and Austria have constantly to seek our cooperation against France and to exert themselves to keep us in good humor."[6]

With considerable embellishment but little variation, this was to remain the core of Bismarck's political rationale until 1866. He wished for Prussia to play the diplomatic game with both hands untied. The two eastern powers should not be allowed to take the Holy Alliance, and therewith Prussian fidelity, for granted. Prussia should at least create the impression that its "good humor" was a commodity on the open market, available to the highest bidder; but such an impression would only be credible so long as Prussia appeared to maintain amicable relations with Napoleon.

Bismarck's letter to William is also noteworthy for what it did not say. In it he betrayed nothing of his enmity toward Austria. It was Prussia's unqualified allegiance to the Holy Alliance, not to the German confederation, which he was placing in question. Ostensibly he sought only to enhance Prussia's diplomatic latitude; what use he hoped to make of it was left, for the time being, unspecified. For that there are at least two plausible explanations. One is that he himself was uncertain as to his objectives; even if we consider that the necessity of an eventual showdown with the Habsburg monarchy was already fixed in Bismarck's mind, there is no reason to suppose that he foresaw the nature, the circumstances, or the outcome of such a confrontation. The other is that Bismarck was perfectly aware of how far his developing views on France diverged from the tradition-bound assumptions of the camarilla in Berlin. To effect what amounted to a diplomatic revolution would require time and tact.

The Crimean War was an important event in Bismarck's career because it largely sustained his personal view of the European realignment after 1848. There could be no more sublime nonsense about the Holy Alliance once it became clear that Austria and Prussia would not enter the conflict on the side of Russia; and there could be no more doubt that Napoleon III was a man to be reckoned with by the time a peace conference was later convened in Paris. The duration of the war, between 1853 and 1856, therefore brought a necessary reassessment of Prussia's foreign policy in which Bismarck sought to take an active part. It must be said that, by his own standards, Bismarck proved to be a rather poor diplomatic representative. In later years, after he himself became foreign minister, he was always to insist that Prussian envoys refrain from pursuing an independent course without the cognizance and explicit approval of Berlin, and that their reports be drafted accordingly. Yet in the 1850's, especially with regard to France, Bismarck's own dispatches from Frankfurt were devoted more often to advocating than to executing policy.

In retrospect it is apparent that Bismarck was remarkably prescient in his evaluation of Napoleon III. In the autumn of 1854 he reported that the French emperor had no intention of provoking conflict with Prussia and that the most likely future direction of France's expansion would be toward the Mediterranean. Napoleon was reluctant to risk any annexations in the Rhineland, since the consequence would almost certainly be the creation of a new European coalition against France. The recognition that Napoleon III was far from being the reincarnation of his uncle was one of Bismarck's earliest and firmest convictions. He was nonetheless bothered by the awareness that there was in Napoleon's person an irreducible element of incalculability. The emperor's delight in doing the unexpected was "virtually a sickness," Bismarck observed, adding that this tendency was "nourished daily by the empress."[7]

From a distance, however, he could not be certain of his assumptions and so arranged for a semi-official trip to Paris in August of 1855. There he had his first opportunity to measure the man behind the imperial reputation: "His intelligence is not at all so superior as the world believes, nor his heart so cold." Yet Bismarck's doubts about Napoleon's unpredictability were not allayed; there was still the Empress Eugénie, the problem of dynastic succession, the not totally accountable pressures of the army and of public opinion. All of these considerations reappeared in Bismarck's dispatches to Berlin in the months that followed. They showed two results of his Paris excursion: first, a keener sense of France as a nation in which a variety of factions and special interests were competing for social and political prominence; second, a reconfirmation of his central assumption about the French emperor himself, that under the proper circumstances

"it could be quite useful to do political business with
him."[8]

As the Crimean War finally reached its miserable
conclusion in the spring of 1856, Bismarck attempted to
formulate a summary of his political views. This he did in
a lengthy personal letter to his superior in Berlin, Freiherr
von Manteuffel. It was undoubtedly the most coherent
statement of Bismarck's outlook on France before his
call to the capital in 1862. His initial premise was that,
however unstable the Bonapartist dynasty might seem, it
was Napoleon III who had now become the arbiter of
European alliances. The crucial sentence read as follows:
"The German *Mittelstaaten* [including Baden, Württemberg, Bavaria, and Saxony] are prepared, now as before,
to join whichever of the German great powers has the
best chance for France's support." Here it was no longer,
as in the 1853 letter to William, a question of Prussia's
part in the Holy Alliance—the Crimean War had made
that argument superfluous—but of an open rivalry against
Austria within the German confederation. Despite
Napoleon's "reserved politeness" toward the blandish-
ments of Austrian diplomats, "the official Vienna press
has not therefore abandoned hope of a Catholic league
with France." There followed a long analysis by Bismarck of France's relationship with the other European
powers, including the likelihood of a French incursion
into Italy and the possibility of a Franco-Russian entente
sometime in the future, "since they have almost no necessarily conflicting interests." As for Germany, Bismarck
judged that the confederation was soon to witness a new
phase of the "historically necessary friction" between
Austria and Prussia. In view of the conviction in Vienna
that Germany was too confining for them both, there

could be "no other way out" than a struggle with Austria. Prussia consequently had every reason to secure the friendship of France.[9]

This summary of Bismarck's general views makes perfectly apparent that his favorable conception of France was primarily a function of his enmity for Austria. His purpose was not to preach preventive war but to persuade Berlin that an altercation could not in the long run be avoided simply by a policy of inaction based on sentimental loyalty to the German confederation. To perpetuate the confederation in its current form meant either to endure Austria's domination or to risk Prussia's existence, and that only "pour les beaux yeux de l'Autriche et de la Diète." Basic to Bismarck's argument was the assumption that the wave of uncertainty induced by the revolution of 1848 had subsided and that Napoleon III had as much interest as any other European ruler in containing the threat of radicalism. The danger to Germany of a revolutionary impetus from France was no longer what it had been before the coup d'état of 1851, nor would that danger recur unless the Bonapartist dynasty suddenly fell. Until such a time Europe would not be the scene of a clash between monarchies and democracies but, rather, a forum for traditional cabinet diplomacy. In that case, Bismarck was convinced, Prussia had much to gain and nothing to lose by an open display of amity toward Napoleon.[10]

In the spring of 1857 Bismarck returned for a second extended visit to Paris where he was cordially received by the emperor and by other members of the French court. His observations were again reported to Berlin in a series of long letters to which he obviously devoted the greatest care. Despite their length, these reports contained nothing that he had not already made quite clear. Once more Bismarck's intention to persuade rather than merely to inform is all too apparent (although he remained pessimistic that his efforts would have much effect on Berlin). For that reason one cannot be positive as to how far Napoleon III actually went in his attempt to assure Bismarck of France's favorable disposition toward Prussia; specifically, there is no compelling reason to assume that the emperor proposed a Franco-Prussian alliance.[11] Certain is only one thing: Bismarck wished to drop a deliberate hint of that possibility in Berlin. If Prussia was to play an active role among nations, he maintained, "we must begin with France."[12]

Bismarck's surmise that his appointment as Prussian ambassador to the Russian court in St. Petersburg represented an attempt by his detractors in Berlin to have him "put on ice" was probably not unfounded.[13] Certainly he had, with his constant heckling about the dubious premises of Prussian policy, given his superiors reason enough to disapprove or distrust his judgment. But if they supposed that he would no longer be in a position to call the decisions made in Berlin to account, they were deluded.

Actually, at his post on the Neva, Bismarck was well situated to comment on the Italian war in 1859, since the question of whether the conflict could be localized depended importantly on the Russian attitude toward action taken by the other powers. Bismarck's daydream that Prussia might exploit the situation by advancing troops as far south as Lake Constance was foolhardy and soon forgotten. His major concern, in any case, was that Austria not be allowed to gain a victory. He therefore began to urge a policy of strict Prussian neutrality on the grounds that Russia would not permit the defeat of France or the humiliation of the Bonapartist dynasty; Prussian intervention in behalf of Austria, he contended, was sure to bring Russia into a general European war on the side of France. An Austrian triumph, moreover, could only have the effect of reconfirming Vienna's domination of the German confederation and of keeping Prussia in the shadow of Austria for a long time to come. Prussia thus had no more interest in a Habsburg victory than in permitting the invasion of German soil by the French. Bismarck's considered recommendation was for Berlin to work for a localization of the war.[14]

The foregoing appraisal was offered to Bismarck's new chief in the Prussian foreign ministry, Freiherr von Schleinitz. To William, now the regent, he presented (in flawless French) a different line of reasoning. An unchecked Austrian advance would force Napoleon III to fight for the very existence of his dynasty and to employ every weapon at his disposal. The emperor would therefore be impelled to stir "revolutionary passions" in every corner of Europe: "Où est le gouvernement qui alors resterait maître de sa politique?" In short, Napoleon was the surest lock on Pandora's box. It is again noteworthy that Bismarck was careful to present his views to William without betraying an openly anti-Austrian intent. Instead, he rested his case on the paradox (for William) that support of a Bonaparte was in reality an antirevolutionary policy.[15]

Bismarck thereby held to the image of France as a basically conservative element in the European constellation. The French intervention in Italy changed nothing in that regard. In Bismarck's view, the general apprehen-

sion about Napoleon's aggrandizing tendencies, raised by
the French annexation of Nice and Savoy, had diminished
all the more any likelihood that the emperor would risk
an attempt to extend his hegemony to the Rhineland. The
result, as he had pointed out before and as Napoleon himself had suggested to Bismarck in 1857, would probably
be to arouse an anti-French coalition.[16] Bismarck felt
obliged to explain to Berlin that he was far from advocating Prussia's unqualified approval of the Second Empire
at the expense of every traditional loyalty. But foreign
policy was not essentially a matter of unalterable prin-
ciples: "I regard it solely by the standard of its usefulness
for Prussian objectives." So far as his own monarchy was
concerned, Bismarck remained staunchly conservative.
Still, it was not his function to question the legality of
political changes within other nations, but to evaluate
"which formation in a foreign country is the most favorable for the strength and security of the Prussian
crown."[17] This was Bismarck's attitude toward the
Napoleonic dynasty in 1860, just as it was to be his response to the formation of the French republic a decade
later.

By the spring of 1861 four years had elapsed since
Bismarck had last seen Napoleon III. It is no wonder,
then, that he felt out of touch with the situation or that
he was uncertain as to what intentions the emperor now
concealed in "his secretive heart." Perhaps hinting that it
was high time for his transfer away from St. Petersburg,
he observed that "it is the great art of Napoleon to
envelop himself in vapor of various kinds so that one can
expect his appearance out of the cloud everywhere and
nowhere."[18] Bismarck's appointment a year later to head
the Prussian legation in Paris provided him with a brief

but crucial opportunity to refurbish his impressions of France. He found the emperor hardly changed, though somewhat slower in body and spirit. During the month of June the two men saw each other repeatedly and found, according to Bismarck, that their outlooks had much in common. Napoleon seemed willing to allow events in Germany to take their course, with one exception: France would not permit a *grossdeutsch* solution in the form of an outright merger of the entire Habsburg empire with the German confederation.[19] Bismarck's conclusion of years before that "it could be quite useful to do political business" with Napoleon was, in his own eyes, sustained; and the emperor was now more than willing. "He had the naughtiest alliance proposals on his tongue," Bismarck reported to Berlin; "if I had been somewhat receptive, he would have expressed himself more clearly." During their final interview, while Bismarck was in Fontainebleau at Napoleon's invitation, the latter went so far as to inquire what William's reaction would be to the offer of a formal pact. Bismarck responded cautiously: "For an alliance one needs a motive or a goal." The emperor was undeterred. He confronted Bismarck with the story of explicit overtures to Paris from Vienna, but he also confided his disinclination to associate France "with the destinies of Austria." From this Bismarck could only conclude that it was above all Napoleon's distrust of the Habsburgs which had prevented a Franco-Austrian alliance since 1852. If so, there was equally good reason for Prussia to beware of Austria as to cultivate good relations with France.[20]

On the eve of his premiership Bismarck had thus already made an analysis of the European pentarchy by which he was to orient his thinking for the next decade.

At the extremities, acting with restraint and as a restraint, were Victorian England and tsarist Russia. Between them, the heartland of Europe was an open field in which all three major powers were attempting to set their neighbors against one another. Each sought a secure position for itself while wishing to avoid an irrevocable commitment to any other. The key, as Bismarck saw it, was in Paris. With Austria France was bound by traditions of religious sentiment and political suspicion. France's relationship to Prussia, on the other hand, was a more straightforward matter of mutual national interest—both diplomatic and, as we shall see, economic. For Bismarck this was an advantage to be exploited. All the more so since he and Napoleon III had one important thing in common: both foresaw the eventuality of a German civil war.

II

THE VICIOUS
TRIANGLE
(1862-1866)

If Bismarck was one of the earliest and most persistent advocates of Prussian rapprochement with France, he was by no means the only one. Nor were the reasons which could be advanced for adopting such a policy strictly political. True, Bismarck's own explanations were ordinarily expressed in the familiar language of international diplomacy. Yet he and many of his compatriots were also persuaded by primarily economic considerations that Prussia's immediate future lay in collaboration with the French nation and not, as in the first half of the century, in conformity with traditional obligations to the German confederation. This subject requires some preliminary elaboration.

No sooner had the tumults of 1848 been repressed

than the Habsburg monarchy began to reassert its leadership in German affairs. This not only meant quashing a Prussian plan for reorganization of the confederation on a genuinely dualistic basis, a matter settled in Austria's favor at Olmütz in 1850; it also involved an ambitious proposal by Metternich's successor Schwarzenberg for a greatly expanded German customs union which would include the Habsburg territories. The adoption of such a plan would have obviously weakened Prussia's leverage with the smaller German states and, in effect, would have reduced Prussia virtually to the status of an Austrian satellite.

The principal issue, and Prussia's chief weapon, was free trade. The political setback to liberalism after 1848 had not altered the hard facts of economic life. With comparatively little capital, few available raw materials, and poor transportation facilities, Austria was interested in imposing a uniform system of protective tariffs in central Europe. Prussia, to the contrary, had a much greater stake in keeping open for export the lines of commerce to western Europe. As for most of the smaller German states, while their dynastic sympathies were attached to a confederation under Austrian tutelage, they had economic interests better served by a free-trading association led by Prussia.

From this it can be easily gathered that the relationship with France was of critical importance to Prussia and that there were compelling economic reasons for Berlin to seek an accommodation with Paris. Although hardly a financial expert, Bismarck was well aware of these matters and did not neglect to add the tariff question to his arsenal of political arguments. Only through cooperation with France, he wrote in 1857, "can we force

Austria to relinquish the presumptuous ambition of the Schwarzenberg plans."[1] During the next few years, while Prussia was still feeling the effects of a sudden economic slump, such advice was tolerated but not accepted in Berlin. The issue was then brought to a head in 1860 by the Cobden treaty, a free-trade agreement reached between France and England. Seeing an opportunity to drive a wedge between the two major German states, Napoleon III thereupon offered a similar commercial arrangement to Prussia. When Vienna countered with the proposal of a mutual defense pact, Berlin seemed to be confronted with an unavoidable option between a French or an Austrian orientation.

Under pressure from free-trading interests at home and from some other member states of the Zollverein, Prussia—despite some initial hesitation—was unable to resist the temptation of reciprocating the French advance. Hamstrung by his pro-Austrian sympathies, Schleinitz was forced from office and replaced by Count von Bernstorff, a man notably more receptive to Bismarck's line of argumentation. By the end of March, 1862, nearly six months before Bismarck in turn succeeded Bernstorff, the preliminary version of a commercial treaty with France had been drafted.[2] To this extent Bismarck's policy vis-à-vis France had already been set in motion before his transfer from Paris to Berlin. The difference was that Prussia would henceforth have in Bismarck a premier who was prepared to exploit the new situation for all it was worth.

The usefulness of the treaty with France was soon illustrated by the negotiations for the renewal of the Zollverein. The Prussian strategy, initiated by Bernstorff and executed by Bismarck, was to make the one agreement conditional on the other. Even the more reluctant of the smaller German states, such as Bavaria and Württemberg, were thereby disarmed and finally induced to accept the tariff arrangement with France.[3] At the same time Bismarck could insist that all commercial regulations be concluded only between France and the Zollverein as a whole—in other words, that Napoleon III be prohibited from dealing separately with the non-Prussian states of Germany in matters economic. This, one of Bismarck's most adroit and significant maneuvers, displayed the pivotal position of France not only in the diplomatic triangle of the great powers involved but in German internal affairs as well.

The emergence of Bismarck as a champion of free trade was not without its incongruity, of course, since the immediate reason for his promotion to the premiership was to neutralize liberal opposition in the Prussian parliament to the monarchy's military program. The details of this controversy are not of concern here. But it should be recalled that William, even before his coronation in October, 1861, had been personally acquainted with Bismarck's views on the desirability of cooperation with France. If the occasion of Bismarck's appointment was a domestic political crisis, then, William and his advisors could have had little doubt as to which option in international affairs the new man could be expected to choose. Fears that Bismarck was prepared to grant Napoleon III important territorial concessions in return for a French alliance proved to be unfounded. Yet the day was clearly past when a Prussian statesman could be counted on to heel at once to an Austrian command.

One of Bismarck's first actions after taking office as

Prussian premier was to return to Paris for the ostensible
and quite unnecessary purpose of submitting a formal
notice of his departure to the French government. He
spent nearly a week in the French capital and naturally
used the opportunity to confer once more at length with
Napoleon. He was then able to advise the Prussian diplomatic missions in the major capitals of his satisfaction
with the cordiality of Franco-Prussian relations, "whose
continuation . . . may be regarded as secured."[4] Through
the vicissitudes of the next four years the fixed point on
Bismarck's horizon remained the relationship with France.
As "revolutionary" as his objectives may have been in
other respects, in this regard his intentions were strictly
conservative. He wanted Napoleon III to stay in command of the French nation and to maintain a neutral posture in German affairs. From the emperor Bismarck expected neither too little nor too much—neither an entente
with Austria which would be intimidating nor an alliance
with Prussia which would be binding. His task was to
hold Napoleon at arm's length without allowing him to
slip away.

The first severe test of this policy was the emotional
and potentially volatile question of Polish independence.
Bismarck was aware of the public pressures on Napoleon
within France to support the Polish insurrections, but he
was—as one who wished both to prevent a French pro-
tectorate in the East and to maintain the sympathies of the
Russian dynasty—hardly in a position to encourage the
emperor's professed desire to play the great liberator. It
was therefore with some discomfort that he received a
French proposal to convene a European congress to negotiate the Polish issue. Bismarck's problem was to avoid
placing Napoleon in any undue difficulty, "above all

vis-à-vis his own country," while yet diverting him from a diplomatic initiative which might force Prussia to take sides against France. Faced with this predicament, Bismarck made two responses of unequal value. The first was to contend that while he himself was quite amenable to Napoleon's suggestion of a congress, it would be difficult to persuade William of the idea (a convenient device to which Bismarck thereafter resorted repeatedly). The second and more substantive argument was that, for reasons of their own, the English were opposed to the congress proposal; surely neither France nor Prussia wished to alienate a mutual friend. Together these explanations proved sufficient to forestall Napoleon without forfeiting his good will. The result was not only to enhance Prussia's credit with the tsar but, equally important for Bismarck, also "to keep France warm."[5]

For all its intrinsic complexity, the Schleswig-Holstein controversy produced in at least two respects much the same result. First, one of the great flanking powers of Europe—in this case, England—was directly engaged in the affair, yet finally withdrew while accepting a de facto settlement favorable to Prussia. Second, Bismarck managed to avoid a hard choice between Prussia's self-interest and a harmonious relationship with France. Throughout the tedious negotiations attending the London conference in the spring of 1864, Bismarck sought to offset the risk of English intervention in behalf of Denmark by encouraging Napoleon to play an "essential part."[6] The ensuing diplomatic deadlock left the way open for Prussian and Austrian troops to occupy the two provinces and force their own terms on the Danes.

There was one important new development in Paris: for his collaboration Napoleon now wanted to extract a price. For the first time the emperor became insistent about the French desire for compensations. Since this was to be a perennial source of conflict in the years ahead, it deserves a special word of comment here. Bismarck recognized that Napoleon's interest in a tangible reward for French support was more than a diplomatic convention or a matter of personal egotism. As Bismarck stressed time and again in his official dispatches and private conversations, Napoleon's position among rulers of the great European nations was unique. The French emperor had neither the sheer weight of centuries nor the dogma of divine right as a basis of authority. The sanction upon which his throne rested, and his alone, was the popular approval of the nation he governed. He could be expected, much as any other monarch or minister, to act solely in the interest of his own country. But one had to appreciate the particular pressures to which any ruler of the French nation, whatever his title, was submitted. Napoleon was the prisoner as well as the profiteer of a national history which had no parallel among the major states of Europe.

For the time being Bismarck sought to mollify the emperor by suggesting a meeting with William. He hoped thereby to offer Napoleon some public assurance, in the form of an eminently newsworthy ceremony, that there could be no more question of a Holy Alliance which excluded France. Before long Bismarck's proposal had escalated into the possibility of a gathering of all four continental sovereigns. When nothing came of this, the matter of compensation for France was left in discreet silence, deferred but certainly not forgotten.[7] Although Bismarck was uneasy about Napoleon's disappointment, he was not nearly so alarmed as his ambassador in Paris, Robert von der Goltz. According to Goltz, the French were not only intriguing daily at the southern German courts, there were also indications of renewed cordiality with Vienna which might be the prelude to a Franco-Austrian alliance. Should Bismarck not intervene at once to offer Napoleon a secret treaty with Prussia? Presumably this would forestall Austria, bind France, and help to appease the emperor's unrequited desire for some tangible compensation.

Such a course of action would seem to have promised obvious advantages and was, moreover, quite plausible by the autumn of 1864. Yet Bismarck's reasons for rejecting it were cogent. In the first place, he calculated that Napoleon did not actually want—or, rather, was not willing to risk—an alliance with either Prussia or Austria. It suited Napoleon's purpose, as well as his character, for France to remain uncommitted as long as possible, ready to intervene at a decisive moment to claim territorial reward in return for arbitration. Secondly, Bismarck assumed that essentially the same would hold true even if Prussia did consent to a secret treaty with France. Such an alliance could at best be no more than an "emergency anchor" which afforded little real security. In a crisis each of the three nations would first tend to its own interests, whatever documents had been signed, and Prussia's only certain resource would be military prowess. Finally, Bismarck professed utter confidence in the superiority of the Prussian army in case of a "decisive altercation." Thus, even without the formal assurance of French neutrality, Bismarck felt that Prussia was ready for "any eventuality."[8]

It is impossible to say precisely when Bismarck became convinced that war with Austria was unavoidable, but it was apparently no later than the summer of 1865. Still, his policy remained as before: to avoid precipitating a conflict while yet not flinching at the likely consequences of a crisis. At a meeting of the royal council in May he therefore advised a policy of caution despite his conviction that "sooner or later" an armed confrontation with Austria could "hardly be avoided." As much as anything this attitude was a reflection of Bismarck's own temperament, a mixture of obstinance and fatalism, one reinforcing the other.[9]

Certainly one should not exaggerate either his prescience or his domination of the ensuing events. In fact it required all of Bismarck's considerable skill to prevent the French from forcing his hand out of sheer nervous tension. The conclusion of the Gastein treaty (regulating the Schleswig-Holstein question) between Prussia and Austria in August, 1865, came as a "painful surprise" to Napoleon and his anxious advisers. The most outspoken of these, the foreign minister Drouyn de Lhuys, criticized the treaty bitterly and openly as anti-French in intent, again raising the phantom of a Holy Alliance. Bismarck was incensed and called Drouyn's outburst a "crude mistake." But he was quick to confide to the French that the arrangement with Austria was only "provisional"—as indeed it proved to be—and to promise that Prussia would support France "everywhere in the world where French is spoken." Even when Napoleon dutifully apologized for Drouyn, Bismarck nonetheless remained concerned that the emperor was badly miffed at Prussia's inconstancy.[10]

These circumstances help to explain the motivation for Bismarck's famous and still controversial excursion to

Biarritz in October. He went there not only to see Napoleon but to be seen, not so much to gain reassurances as to
give them. Despite the Gastein treaty he still hoped "to
keep France warm," to restore Napoleon's confidence in
Prussia while promising him as little as possible in return.
Bismarck's intentions toward France were thus the same
as they had been since 1862: not to alienate Napoleon and
yet not to strike a binding agreement with him that might
cost Prussia an unacceptable price. Above all, Bismarck
was reluctant to allow the impression to gain footing that
he was willing to trade German territory in return for
French neutrality. If the two men actually discussed a
precise bargain, then, the conversation could only have
been delicate, not to say embarrassing, for Bismarck. He
preferred in an unspecified future "to derive mutual
advantage from events which might present themselves
unsought." Drouyn, who saw Bismarck in Paris both
before and after the Biarritz meeting, correctly observed
that the Prussian minister was "buttoned up." After all,
in Biarritz he had gained what he wanted: not an alliance
with France but a renewal of Napoleon's interest in an
alliance. To a member of his staff Bismarck summed up
the results of his trip with obvious satisfaction: Napoleon
III was "ready to dance the cotillion with us without
being sure in advance what figures are included or when
it will begin."[11]

By the beginning of 1866 the political settlement in
Austrian-occupied Holstein was already deteriorating, a
fact for which Bismarck was not altogether blameless.
The annoyance with this in Vienna was such that the
Austrian government firmly resolved "to show its
teeth."[12] In Berlin the feeling was mutual. On the last day
of February William again convened in royal council his

principal civilian and military advisers. While Bismarck still wished to delay any overtly hostile action by Prussia, he was no longer making any bones about his view that a war was imminent: there could be "no doubt" that it was "only a matter of time."[13] Thus the moment had come to raise Napoleon's level of expectation. At their last farewell (in St. Cloud, just after the conference in Biarritz) the emperor had proferred to Bismarck "an invitation to write him confidentially as soon as circumstances appeared to indicate the need for a more intimate and more special entente between our two governments." Bismarck now notified Napoleon, "Ce moment je le crois venu."[14] Napoleon responded to this and to a private letter from William with an unequivocal promise of French neutrality, yet without specifying the reward he anticipated in return. Subsequent hints that France desired compensations "vers le Rhin" were more probably evidence of the emperor's confusion and uncertainty than an indication of some grand design for the annexation of German territory.[15]

Bismarck's astute handling of the French contrasted strikingly with the more desperate policy of Vienna. In early June the Austrian government went so far as to sign a secret treaty with France which promised Venetia to Napoleon as a prize for his neutrality in case of an Austro-Prussian war. This was augmented with an oral agreement by Austria to permit the creation of an independent German state in the Rhineland which, while not formally attached to France, was certain to lie under heavy French influence once Prussia was militarily crushed. From all indications this was considered by Napoleon to be the most likely outcome of a conflict in Germany, and that may account in part for his hesitancy to press Bismarck for a prior commitment of compensations. His failure to do so, at any rate, was soon to leave him empty-handed.

It is perhaps inconsequential to ask what price Bismarck would actually have been willing to pay for a French alliance had the war with Austria not begun in the summer of 1866. The point is that he had done his utmost to maintain the vicious triangle until the last possible moment. The war then spared him the trouble of reconsidering his primary assumptions. Whether he had counted on a military solution from the beginning or not, he had in any case wanted to coerce Austria, and war was only the logical extension of his diplomacy. Bismarck had performed his part expertly. The rest was up to the Prussian army.

In most respects the remarkable military victory of 1866 merely ratified Prussia's gains of the previous four years. Since coming to the premiership Bismarck had secured both a commercial arrangement with France and, on the basis of free trade, a renewal of the Zollverein. These had undercut the protectionist project of Austria for a central European customs union. The effect of this, in turn, had been to splinter liberal opposition to the crown within Prussia and to divide the allegiance of the smaller German states within the confederation. Diplomatic crises involving Russia and England had been managed without producing a serious rupture with either. Thus the chessboard (to use Bismarck's favorite image) had been carefully set so that the Prussians could achieve checkmate with one swift move.

III

SADOWA
TO SEDAN
(1866-1870)

It would be accurate to say that every one of the major states in Europe had the satisfaction of obtaining what it wanted when the war of 1866 began. England and Russia were determined to remain neutral, and did so. Prussia and Austria were straining at the leash, and were released. As for France, Napoleon responded precisely as he said he would by remaining impartial until "extraordinary circumstances" impelled him to intercede. The Prussian triumph at Sadowa was certainly extraordinary enough, and he was now prepared to abandon his "role of complete abstention." But what action should he take? His foreign minister Drouyn and the Empress Eugénie urged a French mobilization on the Rhenish frontier; but public opinion, though largely hostile to Prussia, was set against yet another imperial adventure. Bound, moreover, by his own doctrine of national self-determination, Napoleon finally hesitated to undertake more than a diplomatic mediation.[1]

Bismarck was driven less by a fear of French military intervention, which he had reason to believe could not be effective, than by the desire to have French diplomatic pressure applied to Austria and the neutrals in order to achieve a rapid and uncontested armistice. For him the immediate objective lay in northern Germany rather than in Vienna. He consequently found Napoleon easier to manage than William, whose sudden wrath against Austria forced Bismarck (by his own embroidered account) to resort to histrionics to get his way.[2] Vienna was left untouched and negotiations for a preliminary peace began at once.

To Paris Bismarck began to talk enticingly of compensations, not excluding some German territory, provided he could obtain the approval of William and the Prussian parliament. The French were quick to take this bait and at last set themselves to deciding just what their demands should be. But they were not rapid enough. The truce of Nikolsburg was signed with Austria on July 26, and Bismarck no longer needed to reward France for services already rendered. From this moment on Bismarck was adamant, hardly less so than William, that no German territory should be relinquished. It was now Bismarck's turn to play on Napoleon's favorite theme of national self-determination; he warned that he might unleash "a nationalist insurrection" in Germany and central Europe should the French adopt "a threatening attitude."[3] We cannot know whether he was actually prepared to risk such a gamble in 1866, since Napoleon wisely decided not to test his nerve.

Yet it should be emphasized that Bismarck's appropriation of the nationalist cause—much like his advocacy of free-trade policies a decade earlier—was more than a convenient fiction for consumption in foreign capitals. Although his first priority was clearly to assimiliate three million or more non-Prussians in the north, he was already casting his eye toward what he henceforth called "southern Germany."[4] The view that as of 1866 Bismarck had no vision of a united Germany has been cleverly argued but is, finally, unconvincing.

In all his complex dealings with the French between the battle of Sadowa and the provisional treaty of Nikolsburg three weeks later, Bismarck insisted on one crucial distinction: he would accept Napoleon's diplomatic mediation but not tolerate his political "interference" in German affairs.[5] It is doubtful that the emperor immediately grasped the point of this. He still flattered himself that he had saved Austria; but for Bismarck Austria no longer counted as part of the German nation. The southern German states were not to be a no-man's land between competing powers. Instead, they were to have a special relationship to the North German confederation, the final terms of which remained to be regulated. Concerning this arrangement the non-German dynasties of France and Austria should have nothing to say. That was the sense for Bismarck of the settlement concluded at Prague in August, and it epitomized his policy toward France thereafter.

This still left open the question of compensation. Suggestions had been made by various French officials about a restoration of the 1814 boundary (including at least a part of the Palatinate), about the creation of a small buffer state in the Rhineland, and about the outright annexation of Luxemburg and perhaps Belgium by France. Only the third of these possibilities was seriously entertained by Bismarck after July, 1866. For the abandonment of any German territory, as he advised Goltz in Paris, he had "not the slightest hope" of securing William's consent.[6] That was to say, of course, that he had not the slightest intention of seeking it. His strategy toward France for the next few years was to be firm: not to deny the legitimacy of Napoleon's ambitions but to grant him satisfaction no sooner and no more than necessary, while making the emperor appear as greedy as possible. Bismarck's well-advertised irritation with the forward manner of the impulsive French ambassador in Berlin, Benedetti, has to be understood in this context. Actually Benedetti was the ideal French emissary for Bismarck's purposes, since he repeatedly provided the Prussians with an opening to chide Napoleon about the untoward aggressiveness of French diplomacy.[7]

Bismarck's willingness to approve the Main boundary in 1866 stemmed from his confidence that time was on Prussia's side. His task would be to hold the French at bay while circumstances were working toward the voluntary adherence of the southern states to political unification with the north. He was aware that Napoleon regarded the prevention of German unity as a vital national interest of France. It was therefore both to placate the French and to soothe the apprehensions of South German particularists that Bismarck agreed at Prague to the international guarantee of an independent confederation of southern states. This did not alter his persuasion, however, that the arrangement could only be an interim stage in Germany's national development. There was no truce of mystical destiny in Bismarck's attitude. He simply recognized that the lack of final unification would represent a standing invitation to French interference. The balance of power would henceforth teeter on the question whether the southern states might gravitate toward a semi-autonomous partnership in a Catholic entente with France and Austria, or whether they would join with the north in a federalist national state. If those were indeed the alternatives, there could be no question as to how Prussian interests should be served.

The means by which Bismarck hoped to coax the southern states toward a political union were several. The most obvious and immediate of these was to sustain their need for military protection; and for this purpose Napoleon's demands for compensation provided a useful rationale. By exploiting the inherent contradiction of French policy—the appeal to southern particularism coupled with the demand for German territory—Bismarck was able to persuade Württemberg, Baden, and Bavaria to sign secret "defensive and offensive alliances" (*Schutz- und Trutzbündnisse*) in August, 1866. These afforded the Prussian general staff an opportunity to initiate exchanges of military personnel and plans with their southern counterparts and to urge the adoption by them of the Prussian weaponry and mobilization procedures which had proved so effective in the previous summer.

Meanwhile, emotionally and physically exhausted, Bismarck himself withdrew to his estate at Varzin where he spent three months in seclusion. Yet already he had begun designing a constitutional draft for the North German confederation. Consonant with his image of the Main frontier as a temporary screen through which the national current should be allowed to flow, he attempted to weave a loose legal fabric of centralist and federalist elements. His finished work, not achieved until early in 1867, showed his concern to consolidate the north under the Prussian crown as well as to assuage the anxiety of southern courts and parliaments about the possible loss of their identity should Germany be united. Only by giving due constitutional weight to both particularism and nationalism could Bismarck hope to avoid frightening the southern states into seeking French patronage and yet to enhance the autocratic prerogatives of the Prussian monarchy.

The commercial interests of the southern states provided a third potential avenue of approach. Not the least significant consequence of the war in 1866 was that the Prussian taler had finally replaced the Austrian gulden as the standard currency of Germany. The headlock of Frankfurt on the German financial market was thereby broken and the southern states were required to turn directly to Berlin for monetary assistance. With their hand thus strengthened, Bismarck and his economic adviser Rudolf Delbrück were understandably eager to have the Zollverein renegotiated between the North German confederation and the southern states.[8] A conference for that purpose was convened in Berlin in June, 1867, and a final agreement was reached in October which provided for the popular election of delegates to a customs parliament. For Bismarck this promised to have two important advantages: the elections would be held almost simultaneously throughout Germany, in both north and south, and the resulting assembly was bound to deliver a clear majority for the Prussian viewpoint. Again the difficulty was, as in military and constitutional affairs, that the natural preponderance of the north might repel rather than attract the southern states. The only way for Bismarck to influence the outcome was by cautious persuasion.

So long as he could be confident that "the task of the national development of Germany pursued by Prussia" was being accomplished by these means, Bismarck had every reason after 1866 to preserve the international status quo.[9] Napoleon III was meanwhile being prodded by his advisers to seize the initiative: to reaffirm imperial authority, to demonstrate French élan, to reassure public opinion, to encourage Austria, and to influence the swing states in southern Germany. The pattern which emerged in the months after the treaty of Prague was therefore one of French challenge and Prussian response. Bismarck's primary objective was simply to dampen every French effort to upset a situation, as he saw it, developing inexorably in the direction of national unification. This was patently illustrated by two of the diplomatic imbroglios of the period: the Roman question and the Luxemburg crisis.

It was the French contention that Prussia and France had an identical interest in assuring the territorial sovereignty of the papacy. The Prussian ambassador in Paris shared this view and repeatedly urged Berlin to make a joint pledge to the Vatican, as the French wished. Bismarck refused. He instructed Goltz instead that he was to treat this "delicate matter" with the "greatest caution." Since Germany was not a Catholic nation like France, the two did not in fact have the same stake in Rome. A distinction would therefore have to be made between formal agreement and a "practical" regulation of the problem.[10] Behind the semantics was Bismarck's recognition that the French proposal was intended to involve Prussia in a dilemma: open support of the papacy would cost the friendship of the Italian government, whereas open refusal would damage relations with the Catholics of southern Germany and strengthen the ultramontane movement there to the benefit of France. After this initial diplomatic thrust by the Quai d'Orsay had been parried in the autumn of 1866, Napoleon personally undertook a second attempt in early 1867. This time he wanted to convene an international conference to arbitrate the Roman question. But Bismarck responded once more with an "evasive and reserved answer." His ulterior reasoning was revealing. Prussia could not afford to place its military treaties with the southern states in jeopardy. "These new bases of total German unification," he wrote to his ambassador in Florence, "would then presumably be lost in the long run; whereas a direct French attack against Germany, without the intrusion of confessional questions, would secure and develop the national community."[11] While he thus had no pressing reason to take any action for the time being, Bismarck's principal concern was not so much to avoid an ultimate confrontation with France, if that proved necessary, as to assure that a conflict did not arise unnecessarily from an issue unfavorable for Prussia.

The same was apparent in the Luxemburg crisis. The longstanding desire of the French to annex the grand duchy—which was attached to the Dutch crown but under Prussian occupation and a member of the Zollverein —was reiterated by Benedetti to Bismarck immediately

after his return from Varzin in December, 1866. As usual
his first reaction was to point out the extreme difficulty of
acquiring William's consent. Beyond that, he accused
Napoleon of demanding something for nothing; it was
too late to regard Luxemburg merely as due compensation for the French mediation at Nikolsburg. The only
worthwhile question for Bismarck was whether permis-
sion for French annexation would promote better relations in the future. Could Luxemburg, in other words, be
bartered for French acquiescence to the completion of
German unification? Suspicious that the French were
only maneuvering "to compromise and isolate" Prussia,
Bismarck was reluctant to grant Napoleon more than the
emperor had offered him before the war with Austria:
benevolent neutrality.[12] Yet, although he repeatedly cautioned against the "ruthless urgency" of French diplomacy, Bismarck was evidently prepared to appease Napoleon and even to assist him discreetly. Two things were
unacceptable to Bismarck, however: either a unilateral
concession by Prussia which might offend national sentiment in Germany or a formal treaty which implied the
"forfeit of southern Germany" and precluded "a German
community at the head of which stands the king of
Prussia."[13] Bismarck was thereby suggesting, in effect,
that the French emperor would have to choose between
his desire for territorial aggrandizement and his wish to
prevent German unification. If he decided for the former,
Prussia would not stand in his way.

Napoleon was still without a concrete concession
when the *corps législatif* convened in February, 1867.
Since his hopes for compensation were undimmed, the
emperor could say little before his parliament except that
German nationalism was a natural and therefore accept-

able phenomenon for France. Bismarck was delighted that
Napoleon seemed to be taking his cue; if so, peace was
guaranteed "at least for the next twelve months." Prussia
would meanwhile have time to consolidate its position in
the north and, he added, "with southern Germany." By
breaking the news to the French of Prussia's military
treaties with the southern states, Bismarck hoped further
to persuade Paris that there was no realistic alternative to
the "necessary process" of German unification.[14]

At the end of March the affair took an unexpected
turn. After private consultations with the French, William III of Holland advised Berlin that he was prepared to
sell Luxemburg, assuming the Prussian crown had no objection. It did. Bismarck exploited the opportunity to
make a public display, in press and parliament, of his government's commitment to the nationalist cause. This
served the dual purpose of expediting constitutional legislation for the North German confederation and of
thwarting once again Napoleon's diplomatic initiative.
There ensued stormy scenes in Berlin (Bismarck *vs.*
Benedetti) and in Paris (Goltz *vs.* the new foreign minister Moustier). The situation seemed acute. Bismarck informed the Hague that war "could hardly be avoided if
the affair continues" and let the French know that, if they
should insist on an alternative between concession or conflict, "our choice cannot be in doubt."[15] Whatever the
personal feelings of the French emperor may have been,
his army was in no shape for a fight. The crisis therefore
melted away in May when, with Bismarck's blessing, an
international conference was arranged in London. In
early June Bismarck and William visited the international
exposition in Paris, conferred there with Napoleon and
Tsar Alexander, and notified the press that peace had

been "definitively confirmed." In private Bismarck remained less convinced that the essential question—
French tolerance of German unification—had been resolved. Prussia would therefore need to keep a "revolver
in the pocket and one finger on the trigger."[16]

Open conflict had been avoided; the cold war continued. Bismarck resumed his growling about France's
"dangerous intervention" in German affairs and accused
Napoleon of conducting a relentless "diplomatic campaign against us."[17] If one were to believe only Bismarck's
version, France had become an incorrigible disturber of
the peace while Prussia remained the steadfast and heroic
defender of German national independence. Napoleon's
state visit with Franz Joseph at Vienna in August, 1867,
had indeed afforded some credibility to the charge of
Franco-Austrian collusion to obstruct "the current of
Germany's national development."[18] But the truth was
that by the beginning of 1868 the current had begun per
ceptibly to shift and was no longer flowing in the direction of unification.

Even in military affairs, where the most concrete advances were registered before 1870, the southern states
responded to Prussia's lead with something less than sweet
reason. At a conference in Stuttgart in February, 1867,
they had agreed in principle to adopt the Prussian system,
but this did not soon result in uniformity of practice.
Many southerners continued to balk at the more severe
discipline, the extended length of service, and the in-
creased cost required to meet Prussian standards. Progress
was consequently slow and uneven despite the adoption
in 1868 of a common plan of mobilization in case of war
with France. It seemed that the more "prussianized" the

southern armies became, the more rabid grew the political opposition.

That opposition was a curious mixture of ultramontane Catholics, *grossdeutsch* particularists, southern liberals, and democrats. What they shared was an ardent distaste for Hohenzollern autocracy. All of Bismarck's astuteness and circumspection in constitutional matters could not disguise the fact of Prussia's overwhelming domination of the North German confederation. As a southern self-consciousness developed, therefore, the Main frontier began to look increasingly imposing in light of the Prague treaty's guarantee of southern independence.

In the economic sphere the separatist undertow was most evident. The growth of anti-Prussian sentiment was already becoming visible months before the elections to the customs parliament in February and March of 1868. The balloting in Bavaria and Württemberg gave a clear majority for the particularist parties, in the Hessian voting there was a draw, and even in Baden the electoral returns fell far short of nationalist expectations. At the opening of the parliament in April, despite an oration by William extolling "the power of the national idea," a southern faction formed to counter the northern bloc.[19] Although tariff consultations in the next two years were not without practical achievements, Bismarck was forced to recognize the failure of economic inducement alone to hasten political solidarity. To the contrary, the particularist tide gathered such strength by 1869 that Bismarck's most crucial ally in the south, the Bavarian premier Hohenlohe, was forced from office. So far as the eye could see, Bismarck's great expectations were fading.

These developments were not unobserved in Paris.

Until 1868 Napoleon had placed little confidence in the Main boundary and, as noted, had been unable to resolve his central dilemma of whether to woo the southern states or to press for compensations. Now, having unsuccessfully attempted to work one side of the street, he determined to try the other. He abandoned his vain demands for territorial annexations and set about to check Prussian expansion. It was this policy of containment, rather than a diplomatic "offensive" ascribed to him by Bismarck, which he sought to conduct after 1868. To do so, he needed to offer the southern states a realistic alternative. French efforts were consequently directed toward the isolation of Prussia in central Europe by means of an entente with Austria and Italy. Although secret talks with these powers did not result in a formal treaty, Napoleon regarded the exchange of letters between their monarchs in May, 1869, to be morally binding in case of a Prussian attack.[20] By this means he hoped to encourage southern Germany to resist Prussian encroachment. His optimism in these matters did not prove to be justified, of course, but for once that had less to do with the absence of a conception than with a lack of skill in dealing with his allies and advisers.

For his part, Bismarck felt once more obliged to seize the initiative. What apparently could not be attained in southern Germany on the basis of military cooperation, legal persuasion, or commercial interests, would have to be accomplished by the traditional weapons of diplomacy. The initial signs were purely verbal: warnings about "various symptoms" of French preparations for war and about the possibility of a "sudden decision" in Paris. Bismarck first mounted a press campaign to this effect and then confided to Benedetti that he personally belonged to the dwindling minority of Germans who still believed in Napoleon's peaceful intentions.[21] After returning from his Varzin retreat in late November, 1868, one of Bismarck's first items of business concerned Prussian military relations with the southern states; the discussion centered frankly on projected cooperation in the case of conflict with France. One cannot infer from this that he actively sought a war; as he put it, statesmanship requires "the ability to wait."[22] But he did need an issue which would engage the southern states in a national cause.

Such was the situation in the early spring of 1869 as the Hohenzollern candidacy for the Spanish throne became an international issue. When Benedetti inquired about Prussian intentions, Bismarck at first treated the matter "jestingly."[23] But he was already well informed— he had sent his banker and personal confidant Gerson Bleichröder on a mission to Spain in 1868—and he was aware of the possible ramifications: not that active Prussian support of the candidacy would necessarily lead to war, but that the French were likely to regard it as a deliberate provocation. If Paris then transformed the Spanish succession into a test of national honor, it could equally well be construed as such in Germany. The question of precisely when Bismarck first made this calculation is secondary; that he did so is incontestable.

One factor which affected Bismarck's thinking, now more than in years past, was the character of French domestic politics. National elections for the *corps législatif* in May sharply reduced the Bonapartist majority (which polled 4½ million votes to 3⅓ million for the opposition parties). There was some speculation that the returns were symptomatic of unrest in France which might erupt in revolution or promote external aggression. Bismarck disagreed. As he saw it, the elections had paradoxically strengthened Napoleon's throne, since the emergence of a strong radical faction would frighten and consolidate the diverse elements of conservatism. The peasant and petit bourgeois majority of the French nation would henceforth rally around the dynasty not because of some vague ideological sympathy but as an act of sheer self-preservation. In addition the electoral debacle of the Legitimists had all but eliminated the most bellicose political faction and thus lessened direct pressure for foreign adventures. To be sure, the imponderables remained: the unstable personalities in the imperial entourage, the excitable character of the French people, the dangerous precedents of discontinuity in the nation's recent past. Bismarck nevertheless saw France's main preoccupation to be the movement for liberal domestic reforms and regarded the inauguration of the Ollivier-Daru cabinet in January, 1870, as a confirmation of the fact. This suggested that France could be induced, after all, to permit the peaceful evolution of German unification. Yet it might also mean that Bismarck would no longer be able to count on a maladroit French initiative to provide a convenient diplomatic complication to be exploited; and despite his self-professed confidence—"le courant de notre eau nous y porte fatalement"—the goal of a unified Germany seemed little nearer by 1870 than before.[24]

Bismarck's decision to escalate the importance of the Hohenzollern candidacy can be dated from March 9. On that day he presented his case to William, playing on the monarch's anti-French feelings, which he had been so careful to spare until 1866. The objection cannot be sustained that Bismarck was unaware of the implications. When the stiffening French reaction was reflected in May

by the replacement of Daru by the hawkish Gramont at
the Quai d'Orsay, Bismarck noted in the margin of three
separate dispatches the single word: "Krieg."[25] Gramont's
public warning on July 6 that the French were prepared
to "do our duty without hesitation and without weakness"
was castigated by Bismarck as "very crude." He promptly
ordered that the German press reply in kind. When
serious alarms emanated from Paris on July 10, Bismarck
remained intransigent and alerted the southern states to an
impending French declaration of war. The outcome was
still uncertain, but the one thing which counted most for
Bismarck was sure: "politically our position would become very favorable through a French attack."[26]

The climactic episode was a paradigm of Bismarck's
actions since 1866. At first he assumed that the impetus of
events was drifting in his favor; from Varzin on July 11
he wired terse instructions to the Wilhelmstrasse: "Allow
to happen whatever occurs."[27] But on the next day the
situation was reversed. In Bad Ems William urged drop-
ping the affair in the face of French adamance. When
the Hohenzollern candidacy was cancelled on the
twelfth, a humiliation for Prussia appeared unavoidable
and the setback for German unification incalculable.
Back in Berlin, confined by acute physical and nervous
disorders, Bismarck could only agonize and plead with
William to return at once to the capital.[28] Then a moment
of inspiration, the clever turn of a practiced hand, faced
everything about. Bismarck's editing of the famous Ems
dispatch on the thirteenth—far from being the culmination of a well-calculated diplomatic campaign—was the
improvisation of a man determined to get results at any
cost.

The French were no less determined. Since May they

had steered toward a confrontation with eyes wide open and with the intention of administering a setback to Prussia, fully conscious of the risk. If Bismarck had initially miscalculated the intensity of the French reaction, Gramont's ultimatum on July 6 left no doubt that a crisis was at hand. Even after the withdrawal of the Hohenzollern candidacy, Napoleon's advisers were not placated; hence the fateful instructions for Benedetti to demand public assurance from William that the Hohenzollerns would desist from any further designs on the Spanish throne. It was this act of nineteenth-century brinksmanship which supplied Bismarck with the occasion to edit the dispatch from Ems. The rest followed. On July 14— until then a date memorable for other reasons—the French cabinet voted unanimously in favor of mobilization. It was a foolish and unnecessary gamble. The stakes were too high, and moreover the rules were soon to be changed. Five days later Prussia and France went to war.

IV

THE CONFRONTATION
(1870-1871)

The debate concerning Prussia's war aims began at once, in mid-July of 1870. At the opening of hostilities much of the German press responded with annexationist demands. These were further encouraged by the first reports of military success and, in August, by Bismarck's own hints to his subordinates and to journalists.[1] The tantalizing prospect of wresting territory from France helped lure the German nation to accept unification under the aegis of Prussia. Bismarck was the beneficiary of this incentive rather than its originator. True, there were scattered voices of opposition to the annexation proposals: the very liberal *Frankfurter Zeitung* and the very conservative *Kreuzzeitung*, several organs of Bavarian particularism and of social democracy. But these strange companions were exceptions, not the rule. The majority of the German press—in the southern states as well as in the north—spontaneously took up the cry for compensation. They required no prompting from Berlin.

Bismarck's motivation in espousing the annexationist cause remains the subject of conjecture. We may dismiss out of hand the suggestion that he was merely capitulating to the pressure of public opinion. He was not a man to mistake popularity for sound policy and, besides, he possessed more than enough means to have mounted an effective countercampaign had he chosen to do so. The hypothesis that he hoped to use the annexed territories as bait in the negotiations for national unification has more substance; but it is not unproblematical, since those whom Bismarck most needed to persuade (for example, the leaders of Bavarian Catholicism) were initially among the most reluctant to divest the French of their eastern provinces. A more likely explanation has to do with Bismarck's relationship to Prussia's military caste. The traditional prize of a cabinet war was territorial conquest, and the generals were still annoyed at being denied the sweet taste of total victory in 1866. Furthermore, the strategic importance of the Vosgesian ridge and of the fortified places beyond the frontier was too obvious to be denied. Indeed this was, as he quickly discovered, the most plausible argument which Bismarck could make both to the southern states and to the neutral courts, a reason which could be couched in the *lingua franca* of nineteenth-century power politics.[2]

Yet for Bismarck there was another dimension. The war with France was more than just a struggle of two cabinets and their armies; it was a conflict between two peoples. This assertion—that the true enemy was the

French nation—now became the central theme of his letters and dispatches. "The band of thieves will remain," he wrote caustically to his ambassador in St. Petersburg, "even if their captain changes."[3] In part this, too, was propaganda intended for the neutral statesmen of Europe —all the better to keep them neutral. But henceforth Bismarck's version of the congenitally aggressive nature of the French nation was, more than that, the central assumption of his foreign policy. France stood accused as the "sole disturber of European peace."[4] In order to ensure international tranquility it was therefore Germany's political and moral duty to render France harmless. Whoever the leader of the French nation might be, he would be obliged at the first opportunity to revenge the mounting humiliations of 1870. In the name of European peace, no less, Germany's task was to deny France that opportunity. Bismarck thus claimed for Germany the right of the stronger. The annexations and reparations demanded of France were not to be regarded merely as an act of dynastic ambition or as the due reward of a military conquest. They represented a necessary function of Germany's commitment to the future stability of the European concert of nations.

The logical corollary was stated in another dispatch to St. Petersburg on August 25: "The inclination of France to seek revenge will remain precisely the same, whether she loses provinces or not."[5] Bismarck's use of the plural was significant. A clue to his specific intentions had been indicated several days earlier when five Lorraine *arrondissements* (including Metz) were attached to the administrative jurisdiction of the newly formed military government of Alsace. Here matters stood on the first day of September when news reached Bismarck in

Vendresse that Marshal MacMahon's army had been defeated and the Emperor Napoleon captured at Sedan. This was, as Bismarck exulted to his wife, "a world-historical event, a victory . . . which decides the war."[6]

The French capitulation at Sedan had not, however, determined the peace. The slender chance that political terms might be obtained at once did not escape Bismarck's attention; but within a few hours he was convinced that Napoleon could surrender only for himself and not for the entire French nation. The two men consequently had little of substance to say to each other at their subdued and awkward meeting in a small farmhouse near Frénois. Napoleon could offer no political advantages and Bismarck was unprepared to discuss purely military concessions.[7]

Who was to speak, then, in the name of the French nation? Bismarck's personal reaction to the proclamation of a republican government of national defense in Paris on September 4 was an indifferent shrug.[8] Certainly he had no urgent reason to consider the new provisional regime as the legitimate successor to the Second Empire, especially after foreign minister Jules Favre's declaration that republican France would concede "neither an inch of our territory nor a stone of our fortresses."[9] That remark alone seemed sufficient to disqualify Favre from any serious negotiations with Bismarck, whose commitment to annexations was already irretrievable. The only other alternative was to allow the French "to stew in their own sauce" for a while. In London and St. Petersburg Prussian diplomats thus received instructions not to award Favre's advances the importance "which an overture made by the French government would have."[10]

Bismarck practiced what he preached. On September

19, presumably at his own initiative, Favre passed through the German lines and was admitted to an audience with Bismarck near Ferrières. Some historians have seen this meeting as a missed opportunity to end the armed conflict, reach an honorable peace, and spare the thousands of casualties sustained by both sides in the months thereafter. Mostly for the reasons already cited, such a view is implausible. Favre was saddled with his impulsive "pouce and pierre" declaration, whereas Bismarck had already informed diplomatic agents of his intention to extract from France the "abdication of Alsace and Lorraine."[11] Favre hoped to pay in cash rather than territory; Bismarck wanted both. The two men were also far apart on important matters of procedure. Favre wanted first peace, then a discussion of the terms; Bismarck insisted that peace could only follow once the terms had been concluded. They were divided, moreover, as to the role to be played by the neutral powers. Favre asked that the neutrals mediate the terms and France observe the peace; Bismarck demanded that the neutrals guarantee the peace and Germany set the terms. One thing they could agree upon: the need to call together an assembly to represent the French nation. But neither was certain how this could be accomplished. So Favre returned to Paris and the war continued.[12]

Even before Sedan Bismarck had requested the German press to admonish all nonbelligerents to avoid "hostile interference" in the war with France.[13] He had reason to be pleased with the initial response. The other powers showed a willingness to mediate but not to intervene. They advised moderation to the Prussian court, but they were by no means prepared to guarantee French terri-

torial integrity. This was the reality which the emissary
of the new Paris government, Adolphe Thiers, learned to
his dismay during a tour of London, Vienna, and St.
Petersburg which he began on September 12. France was
assured of sympathy but received no promises and, above
all, no active support.[14] The Thiers trip was nonetheless
far from useless. While it revealed the success of Bismarck's efforts to isolate France diplomatically, it also reminded the neutrals that they had some stake in maintaining the international pentarchy. Thiers was no
Talleyrand, but his efforts at least posed the question
whether Europe could afford another Metternich.

We know of Bismarck's own uneasiness from his
correspondence. In mid-September, just after Thiers' departure and on the eve of the first conference with Favre,
he had composed two long memoranda for distribution to
the southern German states and to the neutral capitals. In
them he naturally blamed the conflict on France; more
specifically he argued that it was French public opinion
which had forced Napoleon to declare war. Germany
must consequently reckon with "the injured pride and
urge to hegemony in the French nation" and must necessarily seek security against "the *next* attack of the
French." Bismarck hoped to fix two points in the minds
of European political leaders: first, that annexations were
a justified measure of self-defense, and second, that Germany was required to extract such concessions "not from
a temporary French regime, but from the French nation."[15] The latter was indicative of Bismarck's present
quandary. The political disunity of France was altogether
advantageous so long as the war continued; but to accept
a defeat and to sign the peace, someone had to appear as
the acknowledged spokesman of the entire people.

Legally that person might still be a Bonaparte—
either Napoleon III himself, who was now submitting to a
comfortable captivity at Wilhelmshöhe, or the Empress
Eugénie, who claimed to preside over a regency from her
exile in England. Bismarck confided to his wife, and
hinted to others, that he would like to preserve the Bonapartist dynasty if possible. There is reason to believe that
this was for Bismarck a genuine alternative, not merely a
ruse in order to badger the provisional government in
Paris to the conference table. Yet he assured the neutrals
that Germany would abstain from any interference in
French internal affairs: "Whatever regime the French
nation wishes to give itself is a matter of indifference to
us."[16]

This pose of equanimity is not convincing. Actually
Bismarck was occupied daily in conversations with various diplomats and agents in an effort to sort out the eventual choice. The range of possibilities was certainly wide
enough. In addition to his contacts with Napoleon, Bismarck began to receive a succession of more or less
authorized emissaries from Eugénie. The English, who
were apparently more interested in an Orleanist candidacy, sent their own mission. The Comte de Chambord
served notice through a German countess of his avail-
ability to preside over a Legitimist restoration. On the
republican side there were now, besides the original government of September 4, the even more militant views of
Léon Gambetta and his supporters to be considered.[17] As
he settled into his winter quarters at Versailles, Bismarck
faced a decision which he could neither precipitate nor
long delay.

Rivalry among the French factions and pressure from
the neutrals were hardly Bismarck's only problems after

Sedan. As usual he had to worry about managing William, a task made "frightfully difficult" by the kibitzing and cold formality of the Prussian general staff.[18] The reasons for this are not difficult to locate. All the bitter feelings aroused by the dispute over the proper strategy in 1866 had not yet subsided. They were now compounded by an important disagreement about the sequence of military operations and political negotiations in France. According to his own later account, Bismarck had wanted either to bypass Paris altogether or, if the city were to be surrounded, to begin its bombardment and assault at once.[19] The military command, as if relishing the exercise, nevertheless opted for a long and systematic siege of the capital. The issue would not have become so crucial in the winter months were it not for the clash of conception and personality between Bismarck and the Prussian chief of staff, Helmuth von Moltke. It was the latter's conviction that the military leadership should have ultimate responsibility for decisions made once a war had begun and for as long as it continued; in wartime all decisions were military decisions. Moltke saw the objective of warfare, furthermore, to be the total destruction of the enemy's resistance. Bismarck naturally contended that political considerations do not suddenly cease to count once the first shot has been fired; in fact the sole purpose of the military should be to weaken the enemy to a point where he is willing to accept a political settlement desired by the victor. Bismarck therefore sought to sustain the priority of political leadership—that is, his own position as William's chief adviser—and to bring the war as swiftly as possible to a favorable diplomatic conclusion.

A break seemed to occur in the last days of October,

when it was learned that the "Rhine army" under Marshal Bazaine was prepared to capitulate at Metz. The French provisional government promptly dispatched Thiers, who had just returned from his disappointing *tour d'horizon*, to discuss terms. Stopping briefly in Versailles to obtain a *laissez passer*, he traveled from Tours to Paris, then returned to Versailles to seek out Bismarck in the rue de Provence. On the first day of November their negotiations could begin.

The details of the week that followed have been often and expertly recited. It was an unequal battle of wits, partly because Thiers' bargaining position had been seriously impaired by Bazaine's surrender but also because Thiers was an amateur and Bismarck a professional. Had they been left to their own devices, nevertheless, the two men might well have concluded an agreement. Both were eager to do so. Thiers represented a policy of fulfillment; he had grasped the military realities and believed that France should negotiate while there was still an opportunity to retain as much national honor and territory as possible. Bismarck also felt pressed for time; his prior attempts to deal with the Bonapartists had foundered, his relations with the general staff were deteriorating, and his concern about neutralist pressure for a moderation of Germany's conditions for peace was growing. But neither interlocutor was entirely a free agent. After his long sessions with Thiers Bismarck was obliged to withdraw to consult with William and Moltke and then to abide by the decisions reached *à trois*. For his part, Thiers was aware that he could not guarantee the approval of both Tours and Paris.

The issues were complex but perhaps not insuperable. Thiers hoped to engage the neutrals in the negotiations from the outset. Bismarck wished to keep them out altogether and flatly refused even to discuss the possibility of arbitration by a third power. Thiers reluctantly acceded. There was also disagreement as to the length of an armistice. Bismarck insisted that it be brief and suggested a truce of forty-eight hours. But Thiers pleaded convincingly for more time, 25 to 30 days, on the reasonable grounds that general elections in France (which Bismarck agreed were necessary) and the convocation of an assembly to ratify a peace treaty could not be achieved in less. Thiers wanted elections throughout all of France— including the eastern portions occupied by Germany and the western provinces still defended by Gambetta—but he was in no position to insist. These were relatively technical matters. The real problems were the fate of Paris and the question of territorial and monetary indemnities. At the insistence of Moltke, Bismarck claimed that Germany could risk no armistice without gaining one of the forts on the outskirts of Paris and enforcing a blockade of the city to prevent any inadmissible provisioning of the garrison. This would be, as Thiers pointed out, to deliver the capital as a German hostage and to concede what was tantamount to final surrender. As for indemnities, Thiers gained the optimistic impression that Bismarck wanted Alsace, only a small sector of Lorraine around Metz, and about two billion francs in reparations.[20]

Even if the Prussians had been willing to settle for this, Thiers was still faced with the necessity of urging such terms on his reluctant colleagues. His attempt to do so was of no avail. On November 7 the negotiations collapsed. Still, this time the issues had been clearly defined, and the distance between the two sides had been at least approximately measured. It remained to be seen which would strengthen its position for the next round of bargaining.

France was a nation divided yet intransigent. There were three major pockets of French resistance: General Bourbaki's army at Belfort, the Paris garrison under General Trochu, and Gambetta's military and militia forces to the west. Moltke's strategy was, while holding Paris and Belfort in check, to wear down Gambetta. This task was not to prove easy, especially after the invigoration of an initial French success at Coulmiers on November 9. An actual military victory for France was out of the question, but every delay of the German armies strengthened Gambetta and undercut the advocates of an armistice.

The next two months were the most frustrating period of Bismarck's entire career. Since a quick settlement with the French republicans had eluded him, he was again moved to reconsider some arrangement with the Bonapartists which might be made operative at the first opportune moment. There were three possibilities: to convene the imperial *conseils généraux,* a suggestion made by Napoleon himself but obviated when they were dissolved in the west by Gambetta; to reconstitute the former *corps législatif,* an impossibility so long as Paris continued to resist; or to accept Eugénie's proposal of a national plebiscite which would legitimize a regency, presumably her own. As Bismarck considered each in turn, he was constrained by an unwillingness to grant the dynasty— as its envoys had repeatedly requested—territorial counterconcessions greater than he had led William, Moltke, and German public opinion to expect.[21] The general staff was in any case frankly disdainful of a political deal with the French, Bonapartists or republicans, and persisted in keeping Bismarck uninformed about the progress of military operations. While he pleaded for the shelling of Paris to commence, Moltke continued to procrastinate. Furthermore, "the air is again so thick with mediation efforts and negotiations among the neutral powers," he wrote, "that I cannot separate myself from His Majesty."[22] The situation was, in short, spinning out of Bismarck's control. His masterful domination of the contingencies in 1866 was not repeated in 1870.

The bombardment of Paris did not finally begin until the week after Christmas. By then, after heavy fighting on the Loire and the Somme, the military circumstances had turned decisively in Germany's favor. At the same time, however, the differences between William's military and political advisers had apparently reached a total impasse. When Bismarck learned on January 23 that the French provisional government was again prepared to discuss a truce—and would send a civilian to do so—he was therefore more than willing to accommodate.[23] That evening he greeted Favre, who was now commissioned to speak for the republican regime, although he could still not guarantee Gambetta's concurrence. Bismarck had his own problem of gaining the consent of William and Moltke. The next day a meeting of the German war council produced another heated altercation between Bismarck and Moltke in which the latter insisted on the unconditional capitulation of Paris as the prelude to a final crushing campaign against Gambetta. Yet by arguing, in effect, that an immediate armistice could initiate an annexationist peace without the cost of additional casualties, Bismarck was able to prevail. He was then free to hammer out the details of a truce with Favre, who thereupon notified Paris and sent an imploring telegram to Gambetta.[24] On January 29 hostilities ceased, just eleven days after the ceremonious inauguration of the German Kaiserreich at Versailles.

One question was still unanswered: who could represent the French nation when it came to signing a definitive peace? The recent military setbacks had tarnished Gambetta's claim. He fulminated about treasonous maneuvers to extract shameful terms from France, but the intractable truth of German superiority in the field outweighed his policy of *guerre à outrance*. One brief test of political strength was sufficient to break him. He announced his willingness to permit elections but forbade any Bonapartists from presenting their candidacy. On Bismarck's instructions the provisional government at once countermanded the order, declaring such a restriction to be incompatible with an expression of the national will. Rather than contest the issue, Gambetta resigned and, for a time, disappeared. As for the Bonapartists themselves, their leadership had failed to unite and to assert a credible claim to restoration. Bismarck's attitude toward them, as noted, was far from disfavorable; after all, no regime would have been more beholden to Germany than a defeated and disgraced dynasty. But any obvious indication of preference by Bismarck for this alternative would only have further corroborated charges of a dictated peace. It was thus in Germany's interest to allow France to choose freely, and so far a groundswell of popular sentiment in favor of an imperial solution had not materialized. This, rather than the coincidence that a Bonapartist envoy failed to arrive in Versailles until twenty minutes after the armistice was already signed, determined Bismarck's decision to deal with the republicans. Besides, if it was a plebiscite they wanted, the Bonapartists would now have their chance.

Until the end of January Bismarck's policy had been to keep a "completely free hand" with the French. Thereafter he was committed to his agreement with Favre: "An assembly will be chosen within a fortnight; it will be convened in Bordeaux; it will make a decision between peace and war as well as on the form of government to be given to France."[25] Actually, since the likelihood of an armistice had been rumored in France for several weeks, the elections were not everywhere so hectic and haphazard as they appeared. They produced, at any rate, an assembly quite suited to the temper of the nation. France wanted peace and voted conservative. Divided between resistance and resignation, disorganized in the provinces, the republicans could deliver only a fraction of their potential strength. The real losers were the extremes: those identified with defeat and those who still advocated struggle, the Bonapartists and the Gambettists. The Bordeaux assembly had a mandate for peace. Whether its royalist majority also had a mandate for monarchy was a question for the future.

It was indicative and appropriate that Thiers gained election in twenty-six departments. He was a symbol of opposition to the Second Empire, of the policy of fulfillment, and of hope for mediation by the neutral powers. He was "l'homme nécessaire" for a nation full of resentment and yet resigned to defeat.[26] One must grasp the intensity of both these emotions in order to understand Thiers' extraordinary position as the "chief of the executive power" in the Bordeaux assembly. His presence enabled the other delegates to say what they wished and still vote as they must. The central issue was naturally the fate of Alsace and Lorraine. To judge by the oratory, one might have supposed that a territorial concession was impossible. Yet in leaving everything to "the wisdom and patriotism of the negotiators," the assembly was in fact submitting to the loss of the eastern provinces.[27]

Accompanied by Favre, Thiers arrived back in Versailles on February 21. In facing Bismarck again he was obviously at an even greater disadvantage than he had been in November, and it is therefore pointless to mock the effusiveness of his efforts to soften the German terms. Still, he cannot be exempted altogether from criticism, especially since his versions (he wrote four of them!) of the confrontation with Bismarck constitute a self-contradictory and transparent distortion. Thiers' fault was to dramatize his own heroic struggle against the odds rather than to analyze what the odds actually were. There is no indication that he realized sufficiently how relieved Bismarck was at last to have before him someone, anyone, who could plausibly represent the French nation. Not only did this assure that Bismarck, rather than the general staff, would remain the chief adviser to William; Bismarck also knew that any agreement reached with Thiers would be honored by the neutrals. The resumption of hostilities would have terminated, perhaps forever, Bismarck's claim to guide the negotiations. This probably best explains the chancellor's belated personal reservations about the German demand for Metz. There is little question that Thiers' bargaining power was in reality greater than he utilized.

Thiers came to Versailles prepared to forfeit Metz and to accept the payment of as much as six billion francs in reparations. This enabled Bismarck to avoid another

confrontation with Moltke and to make the seemingly
generous gesture of reducing the monetary indemnity to
five billion. The rest was child's play. Thiers' proudest
moment came when Bismarck conceded the fortress at
Belfort, but the truth is that the chancellor was disposed
from the outset, if pressed, to trade Belfort for Metz.
When he encountered no difficulty from Thiers, he was
free to barter Belfort for something else dear to the hearts
of William and the generals: a triumphal entry of German
troops into Paris. Thus the Versailles negotiations turned
not on Thiers' pathetic-heroic performance but on Bismarck's almost effortless ability to appease the Prussian
general staff. In the end, as he confessed to his wife,
Germany had "achieved more than in my personal political judgment I consider useful."[28]

The apparent moderation of Bismarck's attitude
toward France—particularly in contrast with that of
Moltke, who wished to cripple the French nation for a
century to come—has led some historians to praise his
foresight. He was not only wise, they say, in attempting
to sustain the primacy of civilian over military leadership;
he was also prescient in his desire to maintain the
European pentarchy rather than to impose a Carthaginian
peace on France which would have bred disharmony and
a spirit of revenge in the years ahead. But a critical review
of the documentation concerning the war of 1870 per-
mits one to be somewhat more skeptical about Bismarck's
motivations. It is undoubtedly true that he had no inclination to reduce the French nation to ruins. Yet there is no
reason to pose the alternatives so starkly. Germany's latitude in dealing with France was limited, after all, by the
tolerance of the neutral powers. Bismarck's nightmare of
a hostile coalition had haunted him throughout 1870. We

may take at face value his assumption, moreover, that the French would eventually seek revenge for their humiliation, whatever the terms of the settlement. The only issue was their ability to do so. To forestall such an eventuality, Bismarck needed a peace which was both binding and burdensome for France, which would be acceptable to the other nations of Europe, and which awarded Germany a de facto status as the strongest power on the Continent. The treaty of Frankfurt was thus to be as much the product of anxiety as of foresight. Above all, it would bear the characteristic mark of Bismarck's future policy: the equation of European security with German supremacy.

V

THE ERA OF INTIMIDATION
(1871-1878)

The German empire was fashioned in a victorious war,
the French republic by a humiliating defeat. From this
elementary distinction it followed that the decade after
1870 would be one of spiritual as well as material imbal-
ance. Whereas German pride and confidence had been
grandly enhanced, the French people underwent a period of introspection and self-recrimination. The perva-
sive feeling of national disgrace was articulated by the
French intelligentsia, who now tended to regard the new
Germany as a disquieting standard by which to measure
the recovery of their own country. Under the circumstances the Bismarckian Reich was bound to appear to
them as a model of power, method, and above all stability.

France seemed, by contrast, to be in a lamentable state of disarray.

It was naturally in the German interest to confirm and if possible to compound the French sense of futility. Bismarck was frank that his policy was to prevent France from again becoming "bündnisfähig."[1] It is important that this concept be properly understood, since it suggests that the chancellor had no intention to abide by any formal canons of international relations. After 1870 he attempted not only to insulate France diplomatically from the other nations of Europe; he also sought to inhibit the internal development of the French nation sufficiently so that it would be able neither to take the initiative in forming a coalition hostile to Germany nor to become an attractive and reliable partner for another power interested in such a coalition. This objective required that Germany exercise as strict a control as was feasible over the performance of the French polity and economy. At no other time in his long career, consequently, did Bismarck muster such direct and sustained interest in the domestic affairs of another nation. He no longer regarded France as just one more piece in an international game of chess. For Bismarck the French republic was not only to be observed and outmaneuvered but to be deliberately manipulated.

The new *règles du jeu* were set by the preliminary peace signed at Versailles on February 26, 1871. Its ten articles specified the provisional line of demarcation for the German occupation, fixed the sum of reparations at five billion francs, and established a series of regulations for troops and prisoners of war.[2] After ratification of this agreement by the German Kaiser and by the French assembly at Bordeaux, the draft of a final settlement was to be framed by delegations from the two nations meeting in Brussels. Bismarck's notion of these negotiations, however, differed importantly from that of the French. While they expected to engage in a process of collective bargaining, he considered the Versailles document as an agenda of firm conditions with which it was France's obligation to comply.[3] The exacting nature of the German attitude toward the Third Republic was thus indicated from the outset. The parade of German troops down the Champs Elysées on the first day of March was therefore an appropriate demonstration of a reality which the French would not be permitted to ignore. But it also served to heat further the resentment already stirring in the capital.

Before the month was out an insurrection erupted in Paris. As a matter of fact, the onset of the Commune was not without its advantages for the insecure republican regime. It enabled Thiers to resort to a scheme (conceived in 1848!) to withdraw from the city and to regroup the government's military forces nearby, preparatory to a crushing assault on rebel positions. It also forced conservative elements in the Bordeaux assembly and throughout the country to offer support, if only momentarily, for Thiers' personal leadership. Indirectly this meant, in turn, that his policy of fulfillment was strengthened as well— provided, of course, that the communards could be contained and that he emerged from the struggle unscathed. Thiers could always contend thereafter that better terms might have been obtained in Brussels had it not been for the rashness of the Parisian populace, infiltrated and misguided as it was by agents of the International.

Nor was the Commune entirely unwelcome to Bismarck. Insofar as the civil war both deepened political fissures within France and strengthened Thiers' hand against his parliamentary opposition, the communards were clearly working for *le roi de Prusse*. The chancellor yielded to no man in his desire to see the Commune crushed, but not before the French government had been brought to realize its helplessness without Germany's indulgence. Bismarck was willing to offer assistance—closing the blockade, releasing prisoners of war to join the army of Versailles under MacMahon's command, allowing the use of railways to move supplies and finally to invest the city—but only for a price to be paid in Brussels. It was undeniably a case of blackmail. The government was initially reluctant to make a formal request for aid, least of all to sign a written agreement which Bismarck might later use to administer a diplomatic lashing (as he had done in 1870 with documents disclosing Bonapartist designs to annex Luxemburg and Belgium). Thiers reminded Bismarck that "Europe" would never forgive Germany for refusing to strangle the threat of radicalism outright. To this the chancellor retorted angrily that Thiers was violating the prescribed troop level north of the Loire and exploiting circumstances to create the nucleus of an army which might serve, sooner or later, to launch a war of revenge.[4]

Yet the truth was that neither had a realistic alternative to mutual accommodation. Bismarck considered and rejected the possibility of having the German army storm Paris. This would undoubtedly have succeeded in short order, but it would also have compromised Thiers before his own nation and forced Germany to assume the liability of a puppet government, perhaps in the form of an enforced Bonapartist restoration. Through his young deputy Friedrich von Holstein the chancellor also established direct contact with the communards, but except as a source of information this could only be a political feint. At the same time, Thiers knew perfectly well that German cooperation was militarily indispensable and that the French negotiators in Brussels could not stall indefinitely.

Germany's chief delegate in the Belgian capital, Harry von Arnim, no friend of the Thiers regime, advised the chancellor that French recalcitrance could "scarcely be eliminated without an entirely new turn of events." Although Bismarck's own impatience was growing, he displayed no inclination to abandon his support of Thiers and the assembly; they should, however, "to a certain extent put themselves in our hands."[5] He finally determined to intercede personally and notified the French on May 1 that he wished to confer at once. Within a week Favre and finance minister Pouyer-Quertier were in Frankfurt, obviously carrying instructions not to try Bismarck's temper too long. On May 10 a treaty was drafted which settled the outstanding questions, mostly in Germany's favor, and stipulated a reciprocal "most-favored-nation" commercial arrangement (Article XI).[6] The rapidity with which the Frankfurt treaty was concluded suggests that both parties felt they had extracted all that was to be gained from delay. Bismarck had obtained his terms and Thiers had gathered his military forces. The way to Paris was open. On May 21, the day after formal ratification of the treaty, the army of Versailles began the final assault on Paris which ended brutally a week later in the cemetery of Père Lachaise.

On balance, the Commune had the effect of further reducing the ambiguity in Bismarck's relationship with the Thiers government. As he explained to the commander of the military occupation in France, General von Fabrici, Germany would henceforth "recognize only the present regime so long as another does not develop from it by legal means." Whereas Thiers was publicly indebted to Germany and committed to fulfill the treaty of Frankfurt, any other French leadership might be tempted to court popularity by abrogating the agreements and "thereby force us to a resumption of the war."[7] During the next two years Thiers was thus for Bismarck, no less than for the French nation, "l'homme nécessaire"; and Germany's explicit threat to resort to force should the French premier be suddenly upset became the bedrock of the Thierist republic.

Bismarck supported a republic in France primarily because the alternatives were worse. It was not a question for him of an abstract form of state but of one condition and two practical criteria. The condition, of course, was the prompt execution of the reparations schedule. The criteria were these: which regime was most likely to perpetuate the internal discord of the French nation and which was least able to conclude a foreign alliance. The best available solution seemed to be the Thierist republic. After all, a government which had both accepted military defeat and prosecuted civil war was hardly well suited to unify a nation. By attempting to appease the Right as well as the Left, Thiers would probably end by satisfying neither; his regime would thus be no better equipped to attract potential allies than to defy a former enemy. The Third Republic would then be forced to function alone with improvised and inefficient machinery for which the basic motor force was no stronger than the energy generated by Thiers himself. No wonder Bismarck approved of it.

As he made clear to William, Bismarck's intention

was to apply constant pressure to Thiers while yet aiding him to survive. To achieve the desired result it was necessary to proceed with some discretion, cooperating with Thiers' efforts to restore order in France without allowing him to arouse "foolish hopes and dangerous illusions."[8] Whereas the chancellor remained personally aloof, though watchful, often withdrawn to his family estate, German diplomats had daily contacts with French officials in Berlin, Nancy, and Paris. The French were admonished to adhere strictly to the reparations agreement, to dampen the anti-German outbursts of their newspaper press, to suppress potentially inflammatory organizations (such as the *Ligue de délivrance d'Alsace et Lorraine* and the *Ligue anti-Prussienne*), and to prosecute vigorously all hostile acts committed against the German army of occupation. Reluctance to comply with these demands brought dark hints of reprisal, anything from a threat of seizing hostages to a warning of reoccupation of liberated territory or, if necessary, a resumption of armed conflict. To be effective these admonitions had to be credible. Bismarck let it be constantly reiterated to Paris that undue recalcitrance in fulfilling the terms of the peace or any sudden change of regime without his approval might very well force his hand— and if so, "better sooner than later."[9] This was neither a bluff nor an expression of intent to unleash a preventive war. It only showed that Bismarck could not exclude the possibility of actually using force if he were at the same time to sustain Thiers in office and to extract from him a total compliance with the treaty of Frankfurt.

One cannot precisely estimate the effectiveness of Bismarck's policy in discouraging Thiers' opponents, since most of their efforts were half-hearted and self-defeating. Such was notably the case of the French royalists, whose ineffectual attempts to achieve a fusion between the houses of Bourbon and Orléans were repeatedly frustrated. Soon after the outbreak of war in 1870, as noted earlier, the Comte de Chambord had tried to contact William by letter in order to offer his services as the French standard-bearer of European Legitimacy. After this initiative was deflected by Bismarck, Chambord did little more than make himself ostentatiously available, while insisting to the dismay of the Orleanists that the fusionist candidate must renounce the tricolor in favor of the white flag of absolute monarchy. German agents followed this controversy with the greatest care but found no reason to intervene. Not even the seating of the Orleanist princes in the assembly at Versailles caused Bismarck to abandon his reserve, even though their English contacts and clerical sympathies made them in his estimation the most dangerous pretenders to the French throne.

The main hope of the Bonapartists was to persuade Thiers to call a national plebiscite which, they believed, would expose the weakness of both the royalists and the radicals. Bismarck was convinced that this was a delusion, and the results of French by-elections generally bore him out. His view remained nevertheless unchanged that the imperial dynasty would represent "the most useful formation" for Germany after Thiers' retirement. Yet he was unwilling to adopt the suggestion of Arnim (now ambassador in Paris) that Germany actually precipitate this transition while there was still time—that is, before the termination of the occupation.[10] The wisdom of the chancellor's decision was confirmed by the death of Napoleon III in January, 1873, since the result would have been a regency of the unreliable and very papist Empress Eugénie.

The major event at the other end of the political spectrum was the reappearance of Gambetta. By 1872 French by-elections were not only bringing important republican gains; they indicated a virtual reversal of public sentiment. Whereas the original Bordeaux assembly had reflected conservatism of the provinces and militant radicalism in Paris, subsequent electoral returns showed a more chastened attitude in the capital and a growing radical temper in the countryside. There was also evidence of an informal alliance between Gambetta and Thiers, the former supporting the president's Left Center position in the assembly in return for a free hand to abet republican agitation in the Midi. Gambetta's behavior thus appeared to Bismarck to strengthen the status quo and, by doing so, to perpetuate French disunity. He was consequently far less nervous than Arnim about the possibility of Gambetta's sudden accession to power and the establishment of a radical republic.[11] Again, time was to prove Bismarck correct and to expose the fatuousness of the alternative proposed by Arnim. So far as the French succession was concerned, the chancellor maintained a clear distinction between intimidation and intervention.

Whatever faction might eventually prevail, Bismarck observed, Germany would still have to contend with "the ignorant and easily deceived French nation," which persisted in wanting its leadership "to play the role of the first military power on the Continent." [12] Even allowing for some politically useful exaggeration in order to urge his own military legislation through the Reichstag, there is no reason to doubt that Bismarck was genuinely apprehensive about French rearmament. It was not that he questioned the sincerity of Thiers' own repudiation of revanchism, but the current situation in France could not possibly last. Thiers' advancing age and imperious manner made him doubly vulnerable to an act of nature or politics; and the very success of his policy of fulfillment—assured in the summer of 1872 by the final coordination of French reparation payments and German evacuation procedures—deprived Thiers of his aura of indispensability in the assembly. He was meanwhile coming under fire both for being too radical in politics (by edging France toward a republican form of state) and for being too conservative in economic and military affairs (by insisting on the raising of indirect taxation and the reconstitution of a professional army). For these reasons, and simply because they did not wish to tolerate his consulship any longer, many of Thiers' opponents began to mount the search for a successor.

Yet Bismarck continued to reject Harry von Arnim's proposal that Germany withdraw support from Thiers and actively promote a more stable Bonapartist or royalist alternative. He denounced the ambassador's dispatches from Paris as "fundamentally false and dangerous," based on "erroneous assumptions" which were "in absolute contradiction" to his own French policy.[13] Obviously an element of personal vendetta came to dominate the chancellor's assault on Arnim; but that should not disguise the substantive disagreement between them as to how best to deal with the French nation. Bismarck's view was that the German interest could not conceivably be served by assisting any regime to power in France which might eventually gather broad public support, since "with such an explosive nation as the French, the future is incalculable."[14] He therefore preferred to take his chances with a republic, even a potentially radical one, apparently on the theory that it would after all prove to be the form of government which divided France the most.

Still, Bismarck was not beyond advancing Arnim's arguments in order to refurbish Germany's alliances in eastern Europe. To Vienna and St. Petersburg he displayed the prospect of an increasingly radical and aggressive French republic which represented both a military threat and an encouragement to sedition. This cultivated jacobin scare was one of the motivations for the series of state visits during 1872 and 1873 which culminated in the Three Emperors' League.[15] A fundamental calculation of Bismarck's diplomacy before 1870 had been that the Holy Alliance was defunct. Now he willingly collaborated in the resuscitation of monarchical solidarity in order to block France from either a two-front entente with Russia or a Catholic league with Austria. This demonstrated, among other things, Bismarck's awareness that the French were bound to regain some freedom of action and that his intimidation of them would accordingly become more difficult.

On May 24, 1873, Thiers was forced from the presidency of the French republic and replaced by Marshal MacMahon. Not since the Hohenzollern candidacy had a single event caused Bismarck to devote such careful attention to the day-to-day business of diplomacy. He was nevertheless unable to hold Russia and Austria to a common front with Germany in demanding that the new regime seek formal accreditation at the European courts. Instead, the English view prevailed that the status of the French presidency, like the American, was a matter of domestic politics which required no prior confirmation by a foreign power. For this rebuff Bismarck held his ambassador in Paris directly responsible, charging that Arnim's insufficient zeal in maintaining Thiers was an act of insubordination which "without doubt has worsened our political situation."[16] Even though the subsequent trial and disgrace of Arnim did reveal the unreliable and unethical conduct of his office, Thiers' fall can more fairly be ascribed to accumulated internal pressures which Bismarck, for all his skillful coercion, had been unable to contain. If, in addition, MacMahon's effortless succession to the presidency revealed the insolidity of the Three Emperors' League, that was hardly something for which Arnim alone was to blame.

Two other developments were certain to enhance the French freedom of maneuver during the balance of the decade. Obviously one was the termination of the German occupation in the autumn of 1873. The second was no less significant, although its consequences were not so immediately apparent. The elation over the defeat of France and the sudden influx of hard currency in the form of reparations had encouraged a surge of financial speculation in Germany. While the famished French economy was contracting for lack of available investment capital (except, it seems, for the 5% government bonds sold in order to pay off the war debts), German enterprise enjoyed an unprecedented bonanza of soaring profit margins and of newly founded joint-stock companies. But in 1873 the overheated German economy slumped as drastically as it had accelerated, and a wave of bankruptcy plunged the Reich into an extended period of fitful depression. Thus ended more than two decades of almost continuous economic growth on both sides of

the Rhine. The prospect that a vigorous German commercial colossus might dominate France in a free-trading
European market was shattered, and both nations were
soon to withdraw behind protective tariff barriers in
order to repair their damaged economic equilibrium.

The limits of German influence on French domestic
affairs after 1873 were perhaps best illustrated by Bismarck's failure to export the *Kulturkampf*. The passage
of the repressive "May laws" in Prussia coincided with
the onset of the MacMahon presidency and with the increasing incidence of religious pilgrimages in France,
symptomatic of a Catholic revival there. When the
French hierarchy then began to employ the pastoral letter
frankly as a political weapon—the bishop of Nancy
actually ordered prayers for the restoration of Metz and
Strasbourg to France—Bismarck demanded that the
French state intervene to curb clerical agitation. Since
MacMahon's government refused to press legal action
against the bishopric, however, Bismarck could only
resort once again to unspecified threats of reprisal. The
temporary suspension of an ardently ultramontane journal, Louis Veuillot's *l'Univers*, in January, 1874, was no
more than a sop to Bismarck which neither silenced
French clericalism nor provoked a rupture between the
government and the clergy. For a time the matter was
quietly dropped.[17]

Yet Bismarck's fears that MacMahon might wield a
strong hand in uniting the French nation were soon dissipated. He came to see the Marshal, in fact, much as he
had seen Thiers: as the least of French evils. In Versailles
a new deadlock had developed since the May 24 presidential crisis. Whereas Thiers had gravitated toward a
republic while the assembly remained in the majority mon-

archist, now MacMahon became the caretaker of mon-
archism despite a steady republican drift in the assembly.
When MacMahon coolly sent Chambord packing for the
last time into his Austrian exile, after refusing him an
interview at Versailles in November, 1873, only two
possibilities remained in the foreseeable future. Either a
sudden coup de main would bring a Bonapartist or radical
upstart to power, or else MacMahon would consolidate his
presidential authority in hopes of preserving the fragile
chance for an eventual restoration of the Orleanist monarchy. Given the French army's dutiful loyalty to the
Marshal, the former was dubious at best; and Bismarck,
in any case, preferred to gamble on the other option. He
therefore welcomed the assembly's vote for MacMahon's
presidential septennate—not as a political settlement, of
course, but as the perpetuation of French instability.[18]

This was the backdrop for the "war scare" of 1875.
The quotation marks are essential here, since France was
in no condition to fight a war had one been declared, and
Bismarck knew it. His objective was thus not to shake the
status quo but to maintain it. He wanted to retard the
pace of French rearmament, remind the French of German invincibility, and recall to the other powers that
Germany's continued domination of France was the most
certain guarantee of European peace. The charges printed
in the Berlin *Post* and the *Kölnische Zeitung* that France
was engaged in "immediate preparation for a war of revenge" were so patently contrived that the French
foreign minister, the Duc Decazes, had little difficulty in
turning the tables at Bismarck's expense. Despite the
chancellor's earnest denials that he had instigated the affair, he ended by being cast as the bully of Europe who
would not stop short of preventive war in order to retain

his hegemony over the French nation. Decazes was consequently able to assume a posture of offended innocence and to bask in the obvious sympathy of the English, who, to Bismarck's intense annoyance, made a gratuitous offer of mediation.[19]

Not that the policy of intimidation was thereupon abandoned. The final important episode occurred during the so-called *"seize mai* crisis" in 1877. With the time of his presidency running out and the tide of republicanism rising unabated, MacMahon finally decided that the moment for a decisive test had arrived. He dismissed his republican and anticlerical premier Jules Simon, dissolved the assembly, and scheduled parliamentary elections. From Paris came rumors and warnings to Berlin that the Marshal's victory would initiate a conservative coup d'état and a sharp turn toward clericalism. Bismarck responded by informing the French, both through official channels and in the press, that the formation of a reactionary government would lead to war. To be sure, the chancellor made the nice distinction that he was not threatening hostilities himself but only regarded them as the unavoidable consequence "of a dictatorial or monarchical preeminence" in France. One can only observe that by this time the French were fairly inured to such thundering and that most of those who actively opposed MacMahon's campaign would probably have done so anyway. However that may be, Bismarck had reason enough to be "extraordinarily gratified" by the Marshal's defeat and the resulting change of guard in Paris.[20]

By 1878, then, France had become a moderate bourgeois republic in which both the jacobin and ultramontane extremes were held in check and which had yet to find a way out of diplomatic isolation. In Bismarck's own judgment this meant a vindication of his French policy since 1870, though it did not disguise the fact—least of all from himself—that he needed once again to alter it.

VI

CONCILIATION AND COMPETITION
(1878-1890)

It was not entirely coincidental that the consolidation of republicanism in France was a prelude to fundamental changes in imperial Germany. The specter of an ultramontane monarchist restoration had finally vanished. MacMahon no longer posed a threat after 1877, and the new French leadership was openly conciliatory. Even Gambetta was prepared to act, if not always to speak, responsibly. With some confidence in the duration of a conservative republic, then, Bismarck could turn his hand to other matters; and meanwhile he could begin to treat French statesmen more as colleagues than as clients. When the Berlin Congress met in 1878 to arbitrate the eastern question, Bismarck was cordial, almost deferential, in his treatment of the French. He could afford to be, of course, since their eagerness not to be excluded from the talks was undisguised, their own interests were not directly engaged, and their viewpoint counted for little. It was nonetheless to be the beginning, as Paris had instructed the new French ambassador in Berlin, St. Vallier, of "a relationship based on mutual confidence."[1] That confidence was further strengthened in 1879 when Marshal MacMahon was succeeded to the presidency by Jules Grévy, a frank advocate of rapprochement who privately advised an Alsatian friend to abandon the "hopeless struggle" of revanchism.[2] It seemed as though a decade of strained feelings had at last come to a close.

This was only one aspect of the more general reorientation of Bismarck's policies at the end of the 1870's. The accumulated pressures of the decade dictated at least three other fundamental alterations of course; and each of them had an important bearing on the relationship with France.

After five years of persistent depression and mounting dissatisfaction, the Reichstag formally moved to adopt new tariff regulations which ended the reign of free trade and returned Germany to protectionism. Until 1877 German tariffs had been primarily retaliatory, exercised selectively to respond to any duties imposed by other nations. Since this had proved insufficient to lift the economy from its slump, Bismarck took the initiative in advocating a system of both industrial and agricultural tariffs "based on our own needs."[3] One of the chancellor's needs, it must be observed, was to reconstruct a reliable majority in the Reichstag in view of the discredit and apparent decline of the National Liberal party. Another was simply to raise enough revenue to undercut the particularist nagging of the Reich's member states. That is to say, Bismarck acted to untangle a snarl of immediate domestic problems, not from the ideological conviction that protectionist policy was intrinsically superior, that it would guarantee Germany's long-run economic development, or that it was necessarily the best means to regulate commerce among nations. Yet, since Article XI of the Frankfurt treaty had stipulated a most-favored-nation arrangement between France and Germany, the tariff increases could not fail to have ramifications for both and, as a consequence, for the rest of Europe. Thereby began what can only be described as a new age of mercantilism. It should be added that France did not take the same advantage of the opportunities of that age as did Germany. Whereas Germany went on to transform the structure of enterprise and to resume a rapid rate of industrial growth, France continued to resist cartelization, virtually made a cult of inefficiency, and soon lagged far behind.

The shift to protectionism, as indicated, was presaged by the sinking political fortunes of German liberalism. The loss by the National Liberals of nearly thirty Reichstag seats in 1878 made it imperative that Bismarck modify his political strategy. The accession of Leo XIII to the papal chair that year provided him with a splendid opportunity to alter his uncomfortable posture in the *Kulturkampf* and to assail an as yet less formidable adversary, social democracy. By means of a calculating carrot-and-stick policy of social-security legislation and anti-socialist laws, Bismarck aimed to win a new coalition of Catholics and conservatives. The implications of this maneuver for France were less direct but no less far-reaching than the erection of national tariff barriers. During the 1870's, as observed earlier, Bismarck had attempted to involve the French in the *Kulturkampf* by demanding that the republican government repress what he claimed was an ultramontane conspiracy. The result was only to cast the bishopric in a flattering role as the defender of French national honor. Beginning with Thiers, successive regimes resisted pressure to defy the Vatican or to open an internal breach between Church and State. After being bridled during that decade, however, French anticlericalists were free to assert themselves as soon as they could no longer be accused of doing Bismarck's bidding. The campaign to secularize public instruction and the adoption of the Ferry laws between 1879 and 1886 were only the most obvious aspects of a bitter and protracted struggle which finally culminated in the separation of Church and State after the turn of the century.

Meanwhile, the socialist movement in France, at first divided and discouraged by the collapse of the Paris Commune and by subsequent governmental repression, was slowly able to regroup. A new Marxist leadership under Jules Guesde emerged to organize a workers' congress at the time of the international exposition in Paris in 1878; another congress was convened the following year in Marseille. There the delegates were repeatedly exhorted to emulate the disciplined example of the German Social Democrats. The persecution of the latter in the succeeding decade made them all the more admirable to French workers, who began to recover the vitality, if not the factional unity, of a genuine proletarian movement. This was made all the easier by the general political amnesty granted to former communards in 1880 and by the republican leadership's disinclination thereafter to imitate Bismarck's harsh example. It would be absurd to ascribe any primary causal significance to German policy in this instance, but the fact remains that a climate of relative tolerance was created in France which rendered possible the eventual reconciliation of the socialist movement with the republic, especially after the passions of the Dreyfus affair had subsided.

Bismarck's decision to commit Germany to a formal alignment with Austria-Hungary in 1879 was another of his major readjustments of policy. In one respect, of course, the Dual Alliance was only a continuation of the effort to prevent an entente of Catholic powers and thus to isolate France. But this is to minimize its broader significance. By 1879 Bismarck had returned full circle to the conception of a stable European pentarchy—now transformed, to be sure, by Germany's preeminence in the center of the Continent. In this scheme France was assigned a part in the West somewhat analogous to that of Austria-Hungary in the East. Germany would offer just enough support to its two weaker neighbors to maintain their competition with England and Russia, respectively, yet without applying so much pressure as to incur the hostility of either of the two flanking powers for Germany. There was one important distinction: whereas Bismarck agreed to sign two formal diplomatic pacts in the East (the Dual Alliance and the Three Emperors' League), in the West he concluded none. Still, the intention was much the same. Like the Habsburg monarchy, the French republic was to be both encouraged and restrained by German patronage.

For several years Europe was consequently treated to the extraordinary spectacle of Franco-German cooperation. "All our efforts," Bismarck wrote in 1879, "are directed to keeping the current French statesmen at the helm."[4] He ostentatiously supported their attempts to extend France's colonial empire in North Africa and in

Asia. He wished them "a little success" in Egypt and spoke benignly of France's "justified policy of expansion in the Mediterranean." He even observed that the French nation ("thanks to a strong infusion of Germanic blood"!) constituted the strongest of the Romanic peoples and thus naturally deserved to lead them. Neither Gambetta's heralded formation of a *grand ministère* in 1881 nor, initially, the chauvinistic agitation of Paul Déroulède's *Ligue des patriotes* was sufficient provocation to faze the chancellor's relentless amiability.[5]

The zenith of rapprochement coincided with the second ministry of Jules Ferry from February, 1883, to March, 1885. During that time Bismarck actually dangled before the French the prospect of a Franco-German entente, based on their mutual rivalry with England as naval and colonial powers. As if to demonstrate the seriousness of his intentions, Bismarck began for the first time to encourage Germany's own colonial ventures in central Africa and in the islands of the Pacific. That he wished to do so in accord with the French was confirmed by a conference on the Congo question held in Berlin at the end of 1884. There was some talk that a new era had indeed arrived. But a few months later something snapped when the Ferry cabinet was abruptly upset after news circulated in Paris of a military setback sustained by the French expeditionary force in Indochina.[6]

For the seriously altered circumstances which ensued, this single incident in Tonkin can hardly be a sufficient explanation. One of the underlying reasons is not difficult to uncover. From 1877 to 1885 Bismarck's self-professed motto had been, "Dans le doute, abstienstoi." Yet he was neither personally nor politically an abstemious man; and if he exercised restraint toward

France during those years, it was primarily due to his conviction that the republic's "internal weakness" was the surest safeguard of peace and consequently of German superiority.[7] He was correct to observe that France possessed nothing which Germany really coveted; but he also had to recognize, as certainly the French did, that the inverse was not true. Even though it is fair to say that the spirit of revenge noticeably abated once the republic had been consolidated, the suspicion could not be erased that the chancellor's motive in urging the French to seek glory abroad was to divert their attention away from their lost provinces. Bruited by such skilled polemicists as Déroulède and Georges Clémenceau, the charge that Ferry was actually weakening France in Europe and that he was only acting as Bismarck's protégé made the French premier vulnerable at any instant. In an important sense, then, the limitations of Bismarck's policies were set by French public opinion.

The foregoing analysis is compatible with the story of Bismarck's diplomacy told with slight variation in the standard histories of the period. It is possible, however, to pursue an entirely different tack of reasoning which suggests that the ostensible reconciliation of France and Germany after 1877 was much less promising than it appeared.

Should one choose an arbitrary date, say 1868, shortly before the national unification of Germany, it is striking to note the similarities between Prussia and France. Each was ruled by a dynastic regime, their populations and armies were roughly equal in size, and both had mixed economies (of private, communal, and state enterprise) which were enjoying an unprecedented rate of growth. The war in 1870 upset this balance, of course, but it did not predestine the development which the two nations would experience in the years ahead. As we have seen, the euphoric boom of the German economy after 1870 was short-lived; and the result was to undercut any expectation that Germany might simply dominate France, economically as well as politically, under conditions of free competition. The reversion to protectionism and the pledge of alliance with Austria-Hungary were evidence that Bismarck had drawn the appropriate conclusions by the close of the 1870's.

Despite these realignments the new decade did not begin well for the chancellor. The national elections of 1881 seriously weakened conservative parties in the Reichstag; and in 1882 the economic indicators again pointed downward. This, rather than a diplomatic effort to court the favor of French statesmen, determined Bismarck's turn to what has been called "pragmatic expansionism." The more active role assumed by the German state in the 1880's was not primarily for reasons of foreign policy; it was above all a symptom of political and economic insecurity at home. With the invigorating effect of his greatest triumphs already dissipated, Bismarck needed for domestic purposes to generate the atmosphere of another heroic age. It would therefore be incorrect to suppose that the chancellor personally remained a paragon of restraint, except for the one brief colonial episode described previously, and that German imperialism was strictly a creation of his successors after 1890. Nothing was more characteristic of Bismarck's final decade as chancellor, in fact, than the self-escalating combination of dynamic capitalism and political authoritarianism, the twin propellors of modern imperialistic enterprise.

Much is to be said for this view, particularly as it does not altogether exclude the notion that Bismarck's overtures to France before 1885 were genuine. They could have been only tactical, however, since a fundamental commitment to an entente with France was more than Bismarck was ever willing to sanction. He continued to believe that the republican form of government was intrinsically untrustworthy; the word of one regime might easily be broken within a week by the next. He remained convinced, moreover, that the French nation would never offer Germany a friendship secure enough to offset the permanent hostility of England, a likely consequence should Germany opt for France.[8] The interlude of conciliation was thus made possible not by a firm decision on the part of Bismarck but rather by his willingness to defer one. Ferry's fall in 1885 then enabled him to affect an air of resignation and to lament that fifteen years of unstinting effort to placate France had been all in vain.[9]

After some time of attempting to contend with a tenacious liberal opposition in the Reichstag and of permitting a relaxation of tensions abroad, Bismarck thus began in the mid-1880's to revert to more autocratic procedures. A detailed account of his travails in domestic politics is not directly germane here, though it should be noted that he was by now quite accustomed to threaten a revision of the entire parliamentary system. But two tendencies, each of which eventually separated Germany further from France, do require some comment: the more determined action of the German state to bolster the national economy and Bismarck's renewed effort to construct a complex system of international alliances.

It was indicative that German agricultural tariffs,

kept at a minimum of 5% to 7% in 1879, were permitted
to increase as much as fivefold in the succeeding decade.[10]
At the same time cartelization of industry went unchecked, while the state took increasing responsibility for
the extension of credit banking to encourage investment.
The social and political implications of this are not hard
to recognize. The German government was beginning, in
effect, to subsidize large-scale agriculture and big industry, deliberately promoting the concentration of both
and allowing Junker landholders and bourgeois indus-
trialists to form powerful pressure groups. For this development there was no real counterpart in republican
France. The French state undertook no initiative of the
same dimension and the structure of French enterprise,
judged by twentieth-century standards, remained
heterogeneous and outmoded. The relative statistics of
production before 1914 testify eloquently enough as to
the results. What the statistics perhaps do not adequately
reflect is the extent to which German society thereby
retained an authoritarian caste character, for which the
tone was still set to a considerable degree by Prussia's
landed aristocracy. France, under the aegis of middle-
class parliamentarianism, meanwhile evolved toward a
bourgeois society par excellence, while its former notabil-
ity either accommodated itself or withdrew into ob-
scurity. Let it be again emphasized that these diverging
paths were not a necessary consequence of the war of
1870 but rather of measures taken in the two decades
thereafter.

   In foreign affairs the thrust of Bismarck's effort in
the 1880's was directed toward maintenance of the Three
Emperors' League in some form—that is, toward holding
the friendship of Russia despite the alliance with Austria.

At least since the war scare of 1875 he had fretted about the obvious logic of a Franco-Russian entente.[11] France needed an ally, and the most elementary calculation required that it be an eastern power, to Germany's rear. Delayed for a while by the rapprochement with Germany before 1885, the French search was bound to continue thereafter; and since Vienna had already cast its lot with Berlin, the logical candidate could only be St. Petersburg. A Franco-Russian entente, however, was far from a foregone conclusion. The ruling families of Germany and Russia had strong traditional ties, and Bismarck knew how to exploit them. Probably more important was Russia's own inertia and desire to be left alone. For tsarist Russia, after all, the French republic was less than an ideal partner, not just for ideological reasons but also because their spheres of interest were hardly identical. The risk for the French was therefore great that their natural ally might renege in an hour of crisis. The road to alliance was perilous, and the goal could be nothing less than an inviolable pledge of mutual defense. It is doubtful that this would ever have been attained had it not been for Germany's increasingly aggressive hegemony over the European mainland. Not logic but fright was finally to create the Franco Russian entente in the 1890's. Some historians believe that it was Bismarck's greatest diplomatic feat to forestall this eventuality so long as he was chancellor. But the real interests of nations cannot always be altered by diplomatic feats, and the Three Emperors' League contained the germinating seeds of its own destruction.

The climactic year of Bismarck's chancellorship was 1887. At least so it would seem if one judges a statesman by whether he has his way. He was still protected by the

faltering senility of the first Kaiser. He was also rein-
forced, for the first time since 1881, by a secure governmental majority in the Reichstag; with it he won passage
for the most critical legislation of the decade, the new
military septennate. Moreover, it was a year of diplomatic
triumphs, a string of successes such as Bismarck had not
enjoyed since the late 1860's. He displayed the skills of
a master by encouraging the first Mediterranean Agreement, renegotiating the Triple Alliance, and sealing with
Russia the Reinsurance treaty. Each marked a point
against France: the first, by assuring tacit cooperation
with England, checked French colonial expansion; the
second kept Austria in the German orbit and posed a
bothersome military threat to France's southeastern frontier and the Rhône valley; the third blocked any immediate hopes of a Paris-Petersburg entente. The total effect
was to isolate France more completely than at any time
since before 1875. Measured in terms of its own objectives, Bismarck's policies appeared to have prevailed at
every turn.

This is not, however, the only standard by which
they may be evaluated. True, 1887 was a vintage year for
Germany. But granted the luxury of retrospection, we
are obliged to apply the criterion of durability. We know
that Bismarck's achievements did not hold, and we cannot
entirely disassociate the collapse of a structure from the
craftsman who laid its foundations. The year 1887 also
exposed the inherent contradiction of Bismarck's work, a
fissure which could be disguised but not riveted firmly
together.

So far as France was concerned, the dominating
event of the period was the sudden prominence of General Georges Boulanger. After the fall of the Ferry

cabinet Boulanger had been introduced as minister of war
—on the advice of Clémenceau and with the consent of
the new premier, Charles de Freycinet—because he was
considered to be the only candidate "whose republicanism could be counted on."[12] Already distinguished from
the outset by his forceful prosecution of military reforms
and his unusual flair for patriotic gestures, Boulanger's
reputation was further enhanced by one of the more
memorable scenes in French history: his ride on a pranc-
ing black charger during the July 14 review at Long-
champs in 1886. At a stroke he succeeded in embodying
the French nation as it wished to see itself and not, in the
cautious personage of its political leadership, as it actually
was.

For Bismarck Boulanger was both a genuine threat
and a welcome convenience. Since he no longer wished to
encourage any entente proposals from France, the chancellor was determined to guard a pose of studied restraint
toward the Freycinet government; and as his son Herbert
aptly put it, Boulanger afforded him the excuse to do so.[13]
Meanwhile, ostensibly in order to match the quickened
pace of French military preparations, he sought a renewal
of the seven-year army appropriations bill (not due to
expire until 1888). Well in time for the opening of the
Reichstag debate, he saw to it that copies of an alarmist
report from the German military attaché in Paris were
distributed to the Reich's member states. This he did despite the thoroughly optimistic dispatches of the ambassador to France, Count Münster, who assured him that the
republican government harbored no aggressive intentions.
Bismarck's marginalia demonstrated his own skepticism;
what he feared, after all, was not France alone but a
Franco-Russian combination. Yet similar reassurances

from St. Petersburg did not erase his worry either.[14] Herbert was allowed to notify Vienna that "in all probability" one would have to reckon with "an imminent French war" against an army "stronger than our own." A complication between Russia and Austria might afford Boulanger the opportunity to sweep the politicians aside. The French nation would then react more in confusion than from calculation. Boulanger was the "percussion cap" of a potential French explosion.[15]

Boulanger served to make all this talk reasonably plausible, enabling Bismarck to work over public opinion in Germany and to mount his assault on the parliamentary opposition. A less menacing France would not have been so useful. When Münster sent a New Year's greeting to William, reporting the docility of the French populace and the genuine apprehension of war in Paris, Bismarck intercepted it, marked nineteen dissenting comments in the margin, and suggested to the ambassador that he reconsider the appropriateness of such a communiqué in view of the approaching parliamentary debate on the military septennate. Münster capitulated.[16] Bismarck then delivered his famous speech to the Reichstag on January 11, 1887, reiterating his reasons for concern. It might be true that the French nation was quiescent and its present regime conciliatory. But the great commotions of French history had always been the work of "energetic minorities." There were those in France who did not cease to stir the "sacred fire" of revenge, and finally "passions are stronger than calculations." Germany must therefore anticipate French aggression "in ten days or ten years." There was no recourse but to secure the necessary military preparations.[17]

When, scarcely to Bismarck's surprise, the appropriations bill was nevertheless defeated, he had the Reichstag prorogued at once. New elections were set for the next month. To obtain the majority he wanted Bismarck enlivened the campaign with imprecations and warnings. He publicized reports of French purchases of lumber (for the construction of barracks on the eastern frontier) and of picrin (a substance used to manufacture explosives). He put the French on notice that war would result if Boulanger succeeded to the premiership or the presidency of the republic. He found no reason to renounce an ominous editorial, "On the Razor's Edge," published in the Berlin *Post*—the same journal which had sounded the alarm in 1875. To the contrary, Herbert was prompted to write of the "inevitability of constantly recurring Franco-German conflicts" and to stress the danger of "a determined military clique in Paris."[18] With malice aforethought Bismarck thus made Boulanger the central issue of the campaign; and the electoral returns on February 21 were eminently satisfactory. Less than three weeks later the military bill was adopted by a substantial majority.

Therewith Bismarck's immediate objective of thrashing his parliamentary opposition was attained, and Boulanger in effect had already outlived his usefulness. But he was not soon to disappear. Although he forfeited his ministerial post in a cabinet shuffle in May, the general's popularity was spreading in radical and conservative circles alike. Reports began arriving in Berlin, moreover, that a faction of Russian diplomats and journalists was affording him active support.[19] Since Bismarck was meanwhile occupied in redressing the damaging appearance of the Schnaebelé incident, a minor border episode which the French had chosen to dramatize as a German provocation, he could only vent privately his annoyance that

Boulanger was still able to exacerbate a "germanophobia of the French verging on lunacy."[20] It was not unusual under the circumstances that the chancellor's habitual paranoia reasserted itself. He speculated that a secret agreement had been reached between France and Russia, to be activated as soon as the signal came from Paris. Thus even the signing of the Reinsurance treaty in Berlin on June 18 was insufficient to dispel the atmosphere of suspicion and recrimination which increasingly enveloped all of Bismarck's enterprises.[21]

With the eventual dissipation of the Boulanger affair Bismarck had little to do. He had rather to thank Grévy's cool restraint, the general's own hesitations, and above all the internal workings of the French political system. Boulangism was a movement which had never quite succeeded in defining itself. Insofar as it did so, it was a form of "advanced" republicanism, a latter-day jacobinism which sought to revitalize the French nation. The caesaristic reputation acquired by Boulanger was an embellishment once royalist and Bonapartist malcontents began to applaud, and to mystify, the man on horseback. The movement collapsed in 1889 not so much for want of personal leadership as for lack of political coherence—because French conservatives finally had no desire to encourage a more democratic republic. Nor did they, for all their public bravado, really support a direct challenge to Germany which might erupt into open conflict. In the end Boulanger threatened to become a kind of Frankenstein's monster which Clémenceau and Bismarck had unwittingly conspired to create and which neither could control. Fortunately for them, Boulangism destroyed itself.

The real lesson of the Boulanger incident became

apparent in the final two years of Bismarck's public career, after William I and Frederick III had died in 1888 and were succeeded by William II. It was, in essence, that the chancellor could not willfully raise the threat of war for purposes of domestic politics and then expect no one to treat that threat seriously in foreign affairs. The French and the Russians took it in earnest; and so did the young Kaiser and his personal coterie of advisers. Although he was initially willing to defer to Bismarck, William II was convinced that France represented a "born mortal enemy" and that a Franco-Russian entente was unavoidable. Bismarck cautioned him that a preemptive strike would only lead Germany into an "oriental dead end." Even if Russia were defeated, the result could at best be the creation of "a second France" in the East, another nation bent on revenge.[22]

Bismarck's advice was sound, but it came too late in the day. No sooner was he dismissed in 1890 than the Reinsurance treaty was allowed to lapse. Nothing stood in the way of a Franco-Russian agreement, and its conclusion within a few years could hardly be thought a surprise. For this William's self-fulfilling prophecy was partly to blame. But so was the unresolved dilemma of conciliation and competition which Bismarck left to his successors.

CONCLUSION

The encounter between France and Germany was the pivotal event of European history in the nineteenth century. One has only to imagine that the war of 1870 had never taken place or that the outcome was reversed in order to appreciate the magnitude of its consequences. Yet the confrontation was not only military. The political, economic, and social transformation of the two nations was a phenomenon far too complex to be explained as the result of a single armed conflict. The fall of France to the second rank of European powers and the emergence of a united German empire are each extraordinary stories in their own right. In the end, however, they are inextricable elements in the development and later disaster of an entire civilization.

No one would dispute that the dominating figure in the latter half of the nineteenth century was Otto von Bismarck. But again it would be misleading to suppose that the fate of nations depended entirely on a single personality. Bismarck's authority and skill as a statesman are beyond question. Still, it was not he who created the passions of nationalism, who trained and deployed the armies that fought, or who determined the economic and social forces at work. All of these must be evaluated separately if we are finally to make any sense of the whole and to avoid the temptation of equating biography with history. Bismarck consequently deserves neither the excessive adulation of those who have glorified his accomplishments nor the unduly severe criticism of those who condemn him and all his works.

At the outset of his public career Bismarck was justifiably recognizéd as one of the more reactionary members of his social caste. His dedication to the principle of monarchy was firm and his distaste for movements of democratic revolution was highly developed. It was thus entirely in character for him to deplore the proclamation of the French Second Republic in 1848 and to react vigorously at the first signs of radical agitation in the German lands. Then as later he saw a double image of the French nation: a powerful militarized state superimposed on the background of a restless and volatile populace. If he sometimes tended to exaggerate the sharpness of these impressions, they were not solely figments of his imagination. Bismarck became an apt student of French affairs, and his judgments were well informed by a knowledge of French history and traditions. He therefore proved to be remarkably free of current clichés which dictated the response of so many of his contemporaries to the reappearance of a Napoleonic dynasty.

The notion of Bismarck's alleged Bonapartism after 1851 should not be accepted uncritically. To be sure, he and Napoleon III had much in common. Both were essentially cabinet politicians who attempted to harness the undisciplined energy of nationalism. The two men also devised generally similar means to do so, by combining authoritarian procedures with ostensibly democratic institutions. Yet Bismarck did not necessarily require the Bonapartist example to act as he did; and in several important respects, of course, his position was not at all comparable. After 1862 the heart of Prussia's governing process was Bismarck's carefully managed relationship to his king, which enabled him to defy the parliamentary opposition. This circumstance was hardly altered by German unification, which indeed served to strengthen the actual exercise of autocracy by undermining liberalism. For Louis Bonaparte the problem of decision was altogether different, and his chief deficiency as a politician was precisely the inability to establish a stable ruling consensus with his advisers. He was, moreover, increasingly beset by an effective liberal opposition which extracted from him important concessions and which in effect seized control of the nation once he had faltered. It is indicative of the Second Empire that Napoleon III's final attempt to maintain his grip was to resort to his favorite antiparliamentary instrument, the national plebiscite, a weapon which Bismarck never deigned—or dared? —to employ. The chancellor preferred more subtle means of persuasion and coercion. To speak of Bismarck as a Bonapartist, then, is at the very least ambiguous.

The most telling fact about Napoleon III, at any rate, was his rapidly declining appetite for foreign adventure in the late 1860's—especially one which might place his own throne in jeopardy. Hence his hesitancy to drive for an objective, the Rhineland, which was bound to be both hazardous and highly unpopular with the other members of the European pentarchy. After 1866 his stance was primarily defensive, despite the jingoism of the imperial entourage, and his chief concern was to halt Prussian expansion. Bismarck read the signals from Paris accurately and staked his policy on the French emperor's reticence to intervene directly in Germany. Thus Napoleon was the ideal representative of the French nation for Bismarck so long as he remained both cautious and in control. A real danger could only occur when this ceased to be the case, as it did in 1870.

The Franco-German war created a hiatus in Paris which brought Bismarck serious problems at a time, because of his dispute with the Prussian general staff, when he was least prepared to cope with them. It was a convenience to blame the outbreak of hostilities on French public opinion and to cast the French nation as a villainous threat to future European security. The view that Bismarck was genuinely indifferent to the identity of the new French leadership is scarcely worth discussing. He would gladly have retained Napoleon, given the opportunity, but he recognized that any attempt to dictate that solution was certain to be thwarted by French hostility. A republic was therefore the least dangerous and most viable of alternatives, particularly in the malleable person of Adolphe Thiers. Yet to argue that France became republican only because it suited Bismarck's foreign policy is an inversion of the truth. The Third Republic was established largely for French reasons, and Bismarck approved of it *faute de mieux*, not least in order to solve his own immediate crisis of political leadership.

A republic too strong would not have been tolerable nor one too weak so useful. After 1870 Bismarck wanted a French nation incapable of challenging German hegemony and yet menacing enough, on occasion, to serve as a scarecrow in German domestic politics. He consequently exploited the Paris Commune to secure harsh terms and thereafter designed to encourage a conservative republic in France which would honor them. His efforts to influence the French development, however, were unavoidably circumscribed in time and scope. Direct German pressure could not fail to arouse French resentment and resistance. Although still obscured so long as Thiers survived, the limits of German intimidation became only too evident during the MacMahon presidency. As a result, Bismarck was induced to permit an era of apparent reconciliation to begin after 1878.

To define the French response to defeat in terms of a single passion for revenge is to distort the record. After 1870 France was a nation plagued by self-doubt and preoccupied by internal problems. Most of the major questions of the time—such as the plight of the economy, the onset of anticlericalism, and the rehabilitation of a socialist movement—bore only an indirect relationship in the minds of the French to Germany's incontestable superiority. Furthermore, as nationalism in France evolved into a reactionary theme and lost its jacobin thrust, it became more involuted and defensive, a lamentation for the lost cause of monarchy. Even the Boulanger affair was not really an exception to that rule, since it only exposed further the timidity of republican leadership and the reluctance of the most outspoken chauvinists actually to risk another military calamity.

Yet as revanchism dissipated into rhetoric, the recovery of French self-esteem could begin. For this the most striking evidence was the program of colonial expansion launched from Paris and openly abetted by Berlin. The amputation of Alsace and Lorraine nevertheless failed to heal. Not that France was ever prepared to provoke another war in order to recover the lost provinces; but the nation could not easily endure the humiliation of obvious German patronage. This qualified the period of rapprochement with Germany and was the underlying reason for the collapse of the Ferry regime in 1885. It was also the root of the Franco-Russian alliance

formed in the decade following. For France the entente
with Russia was not an expression of intent to defy and
defeat Germany; it was a declaration of independence.
If Bismarck's policies did not make this inevitable, they
did serve to create the circumstances in which it was an
obvious and quite plausible outcome.

With few notable exceptions most historians in years
past, emphasizing (even when negatively) the effectiveness of Bismarck's statesmanship and admiring his diplomatic acumen, have tended to assume the primacy of foreign policy in their evaluation of him. But now a younger
generation, more concerned with social and economic issues and generally more critical of the chancellor, has
chosen instead to stress the primacy of domestic policy.
It is the conclusion of this study that, certainly in regard to France, these alternatives are badly posed. Any
accurate appraisal of Bismarck must grasp the interaction
of foreign and domestic policies and should, in addition,
make a point of their ultimate incompatibility. The needs
of an imperial state, intolerant of genuine political opposition and intent on maintaining its authoritarian prerogatives intact, were not well suited to a diplomacy of international checks and balances. This basic inconsonance
was equally apparent in the violent process of German
unification, the competition with France for the allegiance of the southern German states, the annexation of
Alsace and Lorraine, the war scare of 1875, and the deliberate exploitation by Bismarck of the Boulanger crisis.
The same measures which served to strengthen Prussian
autocracy also provoked fears of Germany's continental
hegemony. The record of Bismarck's success in his own
time speaks for itself. But the eventual failure of the German empire has to be weighed on the same scales. What

Germany achieved primarily at the expense of France in the nineteenth century was paid for with compounded interest in the twentieth.

BIBLIOGRAPHY

As the years pass, the problem of compiling genuinely useful bibliographies has become increasingly troublesome. To draft an exhaustive alphabetical list is of little real help, except for librarians and for authors who want to check quickly to see if their work has been cited. Most scholarly books have extensive bibliographies of their own, making it pointless to name more than those works which present the results of recent research or which have worn particularly well with time. Yet to select is to exclude, and there are unquestionably many worthwhile books and articles which have been omitted in the pages that follow. I have confined myself to about two hundred titles, grouped thematically, which should constitute a practical and fairly comprehensive bibliography of Franco-German history in the latter half of the nineteenth century.

In any discussion of the development of nationalism up to Bismarck's time, it is more than an act of piety to mention first the classic account of Friedrich Meinecke, *Weltbürgertum und Nationalstaat. Studien zur Genesis des deutschen Nationalstaates*, 5th ed. (Munich and Berlin, 1919), now in English translation (Princeton, 1970). This book, marred by an excessive optimism which the author himself later regretted, should be supplemented by the comparative observations of Jacques Droz, "Concept français et concept allemand de l'idée de nationalité," in *Europa und der Nationalismus. Bericht über das III. internationale Historiker-Treffen in Speyer, 17. bis 20. Oktober 1949* (Baden-Baden, 1950), 111–33; and by the critical essay of Wolfgang Sauer, "Das Problem des deutschen Nationalstaates," in Hans-Ulrich Wehler (ed.), *Moderne deutsche Sozialgeschichte* (Cologne and Berlin, 1966), 407–36. The damaging effects of Germany's social and political lag behind western Europe are suggested by Helmuth Plessner, *Die verspätete Nation*, 3rd ed. (Stuttgart, 1959). Of more specific interest is Otto Pflanze, "Bismarck and German Nationalism," *American Historical Review*, LX (1955), 548–66, an article which reviews the pertinent literature and reaches its own sensible conclusions.

Pflanze is currently writing what is likely to be the most comprehensive and judicious biography of the German chancellor, *Bismarck and the Development of Germany*, vol. 1: *The Period of Unification, 1815–1871* (Princeton, 1963). Until the completion of the second volume, the most useful survey of Bismarck's career remains Walter Bussmann, *Das Zeitalter Bismarcks*, 4th rev. ed. (Frankfurt, 1968). Still unsurpassed as a record of the early years is Erich Marcks, *Bismarcks Jugend 1815–1848* (Stuttgart and Berlin, 1909). After following Marcks fairly closely up to 1848, Erich Eyck, *Bismarck. Leben und Werk*, 3 vols. (Zürich, 1941–1944), delivers a sustained liberal critique of Bismarck's activities thereafter; the English condensation of Eyck's work (London, 1950) is barely adequate. Eyck has served as a starting point for the critical reevaluation of Bismarck which has been in progress since the end of the Second World War. This has been anthologized and, in a circumspect introduction, analyzed by Lothar Gall (ed.), *Das Bismarck-*

Problem in der Geschichtsschreibung nach 1945 (Cologne and Berlin, 1971). Representative of the new focus in historical research are the essays collected by Michael Stürmer (ed.), *Das kaiserliche Deutschland. Politik und Gesellschaft 1870–1918* (Düsseldorf, 1970); it is indicative that the average age of the sixteen contributors at the time of publication was thirty-six. The articles compiled by Theodor Schieder and Ernst Deuerlein (eds.), *Reichsgründung 1870/71. Tatsachen, Kontroversen, Interpretationen* (Stuttgart, 1970), are generally more traditional in outlook, though certainly no less professional. As a rapid introduction the student can choose among three brief and easily accessible biographies: A. J. P. Taylor, *Bismarck. The Man and the Statesman* (New York, 1955); W. N. Medlicott, *Bismarck and Modern Germany* (London, 1965); or Wilhelm Mommsen, *Bismarck. Ein politisches Lebensbild* (Munich, 1959). The first is brilliantly written but often eccentrically argued; the second slights domestic affairs somewhat in favor of diplomatic history; the third strikes the best balance while upholding the unexceptional thesis that Bismarck's first loyalty was to the Prussian state rather than to the German nation. Also to be recommended is the discerning portrait of Bismarck which emerges from the latter portions of Hajo Holborn, *A History of Modern Germany*, 3 vols. (New York, 1959–1969).

The onset and immediate consequences of the revolution of 1848 in France have been most recently appraised by Louis Girard, *La IIe république (1848–1851)* (Paris, 1968). The standard work on Germany is Veit Valentin, *Geschichte der deutschen Revolution von 1848–49*, 2 vols. (Berlin, 1930–1931). Rudolf Stadelmann, *Soziale und politishe Geschichte der Revolution von 1848* (Munich, 1948), disputes Valentin's view that a widespread insurrection would have occurred in Germany even without the impetus from France. Both scholarly and interesting are Jacques Droz, *Les révolutions allemandes de 1848* (Claremont, 1957), and Theodore S. Hamerow, *Restoration, Revolution, Reaction. Economics and Politics in Germany, 1815–1871* (Princeton, 1958). The European context is most capably supplied by William L. Langer, *Political and Social Upheaval, 1832–1852* (New York, Evanston, London, 1969). Biographical in slant are Erich Marcks, *Bismarck und die deutsche Revolution 1848–1851*, 2nd ed. (Stuttgart and Berlin, 1939), and Gustav Adolf Rein, "Bismarcks gegenrevolutionäre Aktion in den Märztagen 1848," *Die Welt als Geschichte*, XIII (1953), 246–62.

Three British historians have investigated the Napoleonic restoration: J. M. Thompson, *Louis Napoleon and the Second Empire* (Oxford, 1954); Theodore Zeldin, *The Political System of Napoleon III* (London, 1958); and J. P. T. Bury, *Napoleon III and the Second Empire* (London, 1964). The standard French account is by Marcel Blanchard, *Le second empire*, 4th ed. (Paris, 1966). On the response of various political factions in Germany, see Heinz Gollwitzer, "Der Cäsarismus Napoleons III. im Widerhall der öffentlichen Meinung Deutschlands," *Historische Zeitschrift*, CLXXIII (1952), 23–75. The view that Bismarck's judgment of Napoleon III was dictated by his ambitions for the Prussian crown and hence by the rivalry with Austria was advanced long ago by Friedrich Frahm, *Bismarcks Stellung zu Frankreich bis zum 4. Juli 1866* (Kiel, 1911). This theme is explored in much more detail by Herbert Geuss, *Bismarck und Napoleon III. Ein Beitrag zur Geschichte der preussisch-französischen Beziehungen 1851–1871* (Cologne and Graz, 1959). Unlike Geuss, Gustav Adolf Rein, *Die Revolution in der Politik Bismarcks* (Göttingen, Berlin, Frankfurt, 1957), finally rejects the proposition that Bismarck deliberately copied Bonapartist methods of authoritarian nationalism. The gradual decline of French influence on German politics after 1848 is sketched by John L. Snell, "The World of German Democracy, 1789–1914," *The Historian*, XXXI (1969), 521–38.

The opinion that Prussia's economic preeminence in the Zollverein led to an inevitable political hegemony in Germany was supported by Pierre Benaerts, *Les origines de la grande industrie allemande* (Paris, 1933). Yet the fact that economic growth and political development were often out of phase is pointed out by Theodore S. Hamerow, *The Social Foundations of German Unification, 1858–1871*, vol. 1: *Ideas and Institutions* (Princeton, 1969). The history of Germany's commercial policies is presented at great length and with a polemical bite by Helmut Böhme, *Deutschlands Weg zur Grossmacht. Studien zum Verhältnis von Wirtschaft und Staat während der Reichsgründungszeit 1848–1881* (Cologne and Berlin, 1966). That Böhme's book is not quite the epoch-making event which many at first supposed is demonstrated by the severe critiques of Hans-Ulrich Wehler, "Sozialökonomie und Geschichtswissenschaft," *Neue Politische Literatur*, III (1969), 344–74, and Lothar Gall, "Staat und Wirtschaft in der Reichsgründungszeit," *Historische Zeitschrift*, CCIX (1969), 616–30. Although Böhme has largely superseded three older monographs, each of them still deserves mention: Eugen Franz, *Der Entscheidungskampf um die wirtschaftspolitische Füh-*

rung Deutschlands (1856–1867) (Munich, 1933); Hans Rosenberg, *Die Weltwirtschaftskrisis von 1857–1859* (Stuttgart and Berlin, 1934); and Rüdiger Renzing, *Die Handelsbeziehungen zwischen Frankreich und Deutschland von der Gründung des Zollvereins bis zur Reichsgründung* (Frankfurt, 1959). The best brief summary of this subject is by Wolfgang Zorn, "Wirtschafts- und sozialgeschichtliche Zusammenhänge der deutschen Reichsgründungszeit (1850–1879)," *Historische Zeitschrift*, CXCVII (1963), 318–42.

The background of Bismarck's early years as the Prussian premier has been studied by Eugene N. Anderson, *The Social and Political Conflict in Prussia, 1858–1864* (Lincoln, 1954). On the Polish question in particular and eastern Europe in general, see Hans Rothfels, *Bismarck, der Osten und das Reich*, 2nd ed. (Stuttgart, 1960), and Ernst Birke, *Frankreich und Ostmitteleuropa im 19. Jahrhundert* (Cologne and Graz, 1960). A fundamental monograph is Lawrence D. Steefel, *The Schleswig-Holstein Question* (Cambridge, Mass., 1932). On the diplomatic context, see the more recent accounts of Richard Millman, *British Foreign Policy and the Coming of the Franco-Prussian War* (Oxford, 1965), and Helmut Burckhardt, *Deutschland, England, Frankreich. Die politischen Beziehungen Deutschlands zu den beiden westeuropäischen Grossmächten 1864–1866* (Munich, 1970). The first sharp attacks against Bismarck in France are recorded by Klaus Malettke, *Die Beurteilung der Aussen- und Innenpolitik Bismarcks von 1862–1866 in den grossen Pariser Zeitungen* (Lübeck and Hamburg, 1966). The lost opportunities for maintaining Franco-German harmony constitute the theme of Rudolf Buchner, *Die deutsch-französische Tragödie 1848–1864.*

Politische Beziehungen und psychologisches Verhältnis (Würzburg, 1965). A more specialized intellectual history which treats the same subject up to 1870 is Heinz-Otto Sieburg, *Deutschland und Frankreich in der Geschichtsschreibung des 19. Jahrhunderts*, 2 vols. (Wiesbaden, 1954–1958).

The seriousness of attempts to reach an Austro-Prussian entente before 1866 is stressed by Rudolf Stadelmann, *Das Jahr 1865 und das Problem von Bismarcks deutscher Politik* (Munich, 1933). Some reservations are registered by his student Walter Lipgens, "Bismarcks Österreich-Politik vor 1866," *Die Welt als Geschichte*, X (1950), 240–62. Bismarck's evasiveness in regard to French demands for compensation has been described by Paul Bernstein, "Les entrevues de Biarritz et de Saint Cloud (Octobre-Novembre 1865)," *Revue d'histoire diplomatique*, LXXVIII (1964), 330–39. The conjecture that Bismarck and Napoleon discussed specific terms at Biarritz is nonetheless supported by E. Ann Pottinger, *Napoleon III and the German Crisis, 1865–1866* (Cambridge, Mass., 1966). That the key to Napoleonic policy was the emperor's desire to acquire territory in the Rhineland is maintained in the documentary study of Hermann Oncken, *Die Rheinpolitik des Kaisers Napoleon III. von 1863–1870*, 3 vols. (Stuttgart, Berlin, Leipzig, 1926). This has been contested by his student Gerhard Ritter, "Bismarck und die Rheinpolitik Napoleons III.," *Rheinische Vierteljahresblätter*, XV-XVI (1950–1951), 339–70, who makes the dubious claim, however, that Bismarck was never prepared to concede any German territory to France. Critical of Oncken's thesis, yet apologetic insofar as Vienna was concerned, is Heinrich Ritter von Srbik, "Der Geheimvertrag Österreichs und Frankreichs vom

12. Juni 1866," *Historisches Jahrbuch*, LVII (1937), 454–507. On Austria's role two older studies are still essential: Heinrich Friedjung, *Der Kampf um die Vorherrschaft in Deutschland 1859 bis 1866*, 9th ed., 2 vols. (Stuttgart and Berlin, 1912), and Chester W. Clark, *Franz Joseph and Bismarck. The Diplomacy of Austria before the War of 1866* (Cambridge, Mass., 1934). In his study of the newspaper press Lynn M. Case, *French Opinion on War and Diplomacy during the Second Empire* (Philadelphia, 1954), concluded that France was substantially prussophile in 1866; but André Armengaud, *L'opinion publique en France et la crise nationale allemande en 1866* (Paris, 1962), demonstrates the contrary. Rudolf von Albertini, "Frankreichs Stellungnahme zur Deutschen Einigung während des zweiten Kaiserreiches," *Schweizerische Zeitschrift für Geschichte*, V (1955), 305–68, generally sustains the latter view but notes a "pro-Prussian wave" of sentiment in Paris during May and June of 1866.

The military engagement is succinctly described by Gordon A. Craig, *The Battle of Königgrätz. Prussia's Victory over Austria, 1866* (Philadelphia and New York, 1964). Its political importance is evaluated by Herbert Michaelis, "Königgrätz, eine geschichtliche Wende," *Die Welt als Geschichte*, XII (1952), 177–202; by Wilhelm Schüssler, *Königgrätz 1866: Bismarcks tragische Trennung von Oesterreich* (Munich, 1958); and in the summary essay by Adam Wandruszka, *Schicksalsjahr 1866* (Graz, Vienna, Cologne, 1966). Also see the judicious commentary of Friedrich P. Kahlenberg, "Das Epochenjahr 1866 in der deutschen Geschichte," in Stürmer (ed.), *Das kaiserliche Deutschland*, 51–74.

Bismarck's initial efforts to consolidate the gains of

the war with Austria have been outlined by Wilhelm Schüssler, *Bismarcks Kampf um Süddeutschland 1867* (Berlin, 1929). A detailed analysis of his part in drafting the constitution of the North German confederation is contained in Otto Becker, *Bismarcks Ringen um Deutschlands Gestaltung* (Heidelberg, 1958). Walter Schübelin, *Das Zollparlament und die Politik von Baden, Bayern und Württemberg 1866–1870* (Berlin, 1935), holds that Bismarck had by 1868 already given up on the customs scheme as a means to political unification. On the reaction in Bavaria, see Michael Doeberl, *Bayern und die Bismarcksche Reichsgründung* (Munich, 1925); Theodor Schieder, *Die kleindeutsche Partei in Bayern in den Kämpfen um die nationale Einheit 1863–1871* (Munich, 1936); and the more general perspective of George G. Windell, *The Catholics and German Unity, 1866–1871* (Minneapolis, 1954). The underlying reasons for Baden's support of Prussian policy are explained by Lothar Gall, *Der Liberalismus als regierende Partei. Das Grossherzogtum Baden zwischen Restauration und Reichsgründung* (Wiesbaden, 1968). There is no work of comparable quality for Württemberg. Josef Becker, "Der Krieg mit Frankreich als Problem der kleindeutschen Einigungspolitik Bismarcks 1866–1870," in Stürmer (ed.), *Das kaiserliche Deutschland,* 75–88, stresses that Bismarck's control of the opposition within northern Germany was also in jeopardy by 1870; the conflict with France therefore served not only to complete national unification but to avoid forfeiting the accomplishments of 1866. In this connection see the article by George G. Windell, "The Bismarckian Empire as a Federal State, 1866–1880; A Chronicle of Failure," *Central European History*, II (1969), 291–311.

The French counterstrategy is regarded with some cynicism by Anton Lamberti, *Die Bündnisverhandlungen Napoleons III. gegen Preussen in den Jahren vor 1870* (Würzburg, 1939). But William E. Echard, "Conference Diplomacy in the German Policy of Napoleon III, 1868–1869," *French Historical Studies*, IV (1966), 239–64, contends that the emperor genuinely wanted to settle the German question by compromise, even though he was skeptical about an Austrian proposal of general disarmament. The motive of revenge in the Franco-Austrian negotiations is emphasized by Heinrich Potthoff, *Die deutsche Politik Beusts von seiner Berufung zum österreichischen Aussenminister Oktober 1866 bis zum Ausbruch des deutsch-französischen Krieges 1870/71* (Bonn, 1968). Capably researched, although infelicitously written, is the monograph of Willard Allen Fletcher, *The Mission of Vincent Benedetti to Berlin, 1864–1870* (The Hague, 1965). The culmination of France's internal difficulties by 1870 is treated by Theodore Zeldin, *Emile Ollivier and the Liberal Empire of Napoleon III* (Oxford, 1963). The importance of official propaganda has been underlined by Irene Collins, *The Government and the Newspaper Press in France, 1814–1881* (Oxford, 1959). For Germany see Irene Fischer-Frauendienst, *Bismarcks Pressepolitik* (Münster, 1963), and the far more thorough work of Eberhard Naujoks, *Bismarcks auswärtige Pressepolitik und die Reichsgründung (1865–1871)* (Wiesbaden, 1968). Robert Nöll von der Nahmer, *Bismarcks Reptilienfonds* (Mainz, 1968), gives a disappointing report on a subject which merits further investigation.

The first to reconstruct a detailed chronicle of the events which led directly to armed conflict was Robert H. Lord, *The Origins of the War of 1870* (Cambridge,

Mass., 1924); this version dramatizes the importance of the Ems dispatch and in general is highly critical of Bismarck. Lord's documentation has been substantially amplified by Georges Bonnin (ed.), *Bismarck and the Hohenzollern Candidature for the Spanish Throne* (London, 1957). Subsequently two scholars have all but exculpated Bismarck from the intention at the outset to provoke a military confrontation: Jochen Dittrich, *Bismarck, Frankreich und die spanische Thronkandidatur der Hohenzollern. Die "Kriegsschuldfrage" von 1870* (Munich, 1962); and Lawrence D. Steefel, *Bismarck, the Hohenzollern Candidacy, and the Origins of the Franco-German War of 1870* (Cambridge, Mass., 1962). Harsh in their judgment of the French leadership are Jean Stengers, "Aux origines de la guerre de 1870: Gouvernement et opinion publique," *Revue belge de philologie et d'histoire*, XXXIV (1956), 701–47; Nancy Nichols Barker, "Napoleon III and the Hohenzollern Candidacy for the Spanish Throne," *The Historian*, XXIX (1967), 431–50; and especially Eberhard Kolb, *Der Kriegsausbruch 1870. Politische Entscheidungsprozesse und Verantwortlichkeiten in der Julikrise 1870* (Göttingen, 1970). The tendency to shift responsibility away from Bismarck and to portray the French as victims of their own propaganda is indicated by the second thoughts of Jochen Dittrich, "Ursachen und Ausbruch des deutsch-französischen Krieges 1870/71," in Schieder and Deuerlein (eds.), *Reichsgründung 1870/71*, 64–94. But see the balanced critique by Bastiaan Schot, "Die Entstehung des Deutsch-Französischen Krieges und die Gründung des Deutschen Reiches," in Helmut Böhme (ed.), *Probleme der Reichsgründungszeit, 1848–1879* (Cologne and Berlin, 1968), 269–95.

Incomparably the best general account of the military operations in 1870 is Michael Howard, *The Franco-Prussian War* (New York, 1961). This can now be augmented by the anthology of Wolfgang von Groote and Ursala von Gersdorff (eds.), *Entscheidung 1870. Der deutsch-französische Krieg* (Stuttgart, 1970). Melvin Kranzberg, *The Siege of Paris, 1870–1871. A Political and Social History* (Ithaca, 1950), is brief and scholarly. On Bismarck's strained relationship with the Prussian general staff there is Anneliese Klein-Wuttig, *Politik und Kriegführung in den deutschen Einigungskriegen 1864, 1866 und 1870/71* (Berlin, 1934); the eloquent statement, quite favorable to Bismarck, by Gerhard Ritter, *Staatskunst und Kriegshandwerk. Das Problem des "Militarismus" in Deutschland*, vol. 1: *Die altpreussische Tradition (1740–1890)*, 3rd ed. (Munich, 1965), which is now available in English translation (Coral Gables, Fla., 1969); the expert summary in Gordon A. Craig, *The Politics of the Prussian Army, 1640–1945* (New York and Oxford, 1956); and the meticulous critique of Eberhard Kolb, "Kriegführung und Politik 1870/71," in Schieder and Deuerlein (eds.), *Reichsgründung 1870/71*, 95–118. These authors are all at odds with Eberhard Kessel, *Moltke* (Stuttgart, 1957), who contends in vain that there was no important disagreement in principle, only a clash of personality, between Bismarck and Moltke. On the latter the authority is thus still Rudolf Stadelmann, *Moltke und der Staat* (Krefeld, 1950).

In a battle of scholarly articles Walter Lipgens, "Bismarck, die öffentliche Meinung und die Annexion von Elsass und Lothringen 1870," *Historische Zeitschrift*, CIC (1964), 31–112, asserted that Bismarck deliberately manipulated the German press to produce demands for

Bibliography

Becker, "Baden, Bismarck und die Annexion von Elsass
und Lothringen," *Zeitschrift für die Geschichte des
Oberrheins*, CXV (1967), 167–204; Lothar Gall, "Zur
Frage der Annexion von Elsass und Lothringen 1870,"
Historische Zeitschrift, CCVI (1968), 265–326; and
Eberhard Kolb, "Bismarck und das Aufkommen der An-
nexionsforderung 1870," *Historische Zeitschrift*, CCIX
(1969), 318–56. Long ago Richard Hartshorne, "The
Franco-German Boundary of 1871," *World Politics*, II
(1949–1950), 209–50, disproved the notion of an economic rationale for annexation. Yet an unduly literal
Marxist interpretation is still upheld, somewhat errati-
cally, by George W. F. Hallgarten, *Imperialismus vor
1914. Die soziologischen Grundlagen der Aussenpolitik
europäischer Grossmächte vor dem Ersten Weltkrieg*,
2nd rev. ed., 2 vols. (Munich, 1963), and, more consis-
tently, by Ernst Engelberg, *Deutschland 1871–1897.
Deutschland in der Übergangsperiode zum Imperialismus*
(East Berlin, 1965). The subject has been pursued further
by Hans-Ulrich Wehler, "Das 'Reichsland' Elsass-
Lothringen, 1870–79," in Böhme (ed.), *Probleme der
Reichsgründungszeit*, 431–47, and by Frederic H. Seager,
"The Alsace-Lorraine Question in France, 1871–1914,"
in Charles K. Warner (ed.), *From the Ancien Régime to
the Popular Front* (New York and London, 1969), 111–
26.

The history of the peace negotiations has been docu-
mented by Hans Goldschmidt, *Bismarck und die
Friedensunterhändler 1871. Die deutsch-französischen
Friedensverhandlungen zu Brüssel und Frankfurt, März
bis Dezember 1871* (Berlin and Leipzig, 1929). Thiers'
version has been cruelly but justly dissected by Georg

Küntzel, *Thiers und Bismarck* (Bonn, 1905). The best account of the Napoleonic alternative is still the essay by Joachim Kühn, "Bismarck und der Bonapartismus im Winter 1870/71," *Preussische Jahrbücher*, CLXIII (1916), 49–100. The attempt to update these older studies by Robert I. Giesberg, *The Treaty of Frankfort. A Study in Diplomatic History, September 1870–September 1873* (Philadelphia, 1966), is likely to be superseded in a forthcoming book by Eberhard Kolb, based on his Göttingen *Habilitationsschrift* (1968). The German occupation is described by Karl Linnebach, *Deutschland als Sieger im besetzten Frankreich 1871–1873* (Stuttgart, 1924), and its political effects by Hans Herzfeld, *Deutschland und das geschlagene Frankreich 1871–1873* (Berlin, 1924). The influence of the neutrals is examined by Werner E. Mosse, *The European Powers and the German Question, 1848–71* (Cambridge, 1958), and by Klaus Hildebrand, "Von der Reichseinigung zur 'Krieg-in-Sicht'-Krise. Preussen-Deutschland als Faktor der britischen Aussen-politik 1866–1875," in Stürmer (ed.), *Das kaiserliche Deutschland*, 205–34; both concentrate on the rivalry of England and Russia.

The proclamation of Germany's imperial status in the Hall of Mirrors is narrated by Gustav Adolf Rein, *Die Reichsgründung in Versailles, 18. Januar 1871* (Munich, 1958). A more penetrating evaluation is given by Theodor Schieder, *Das deutsche Kaiserreich von 1871 als Nationalstaat* (Cologne and Opladen, 1961). The massive commentary by Ernst Rudolf Huber, *Deutsche Verfassungsgeschichte seit 1789*, 4 vols. (Stuttgart, 1957–1969), generously presents the Bismarckian system as a characteristically German variant of western European constitutional monarchy. See the critique of this view by

Hans Boldt, "Deutscher Konstitutionalismus und Bismarckreich," in Stürmer (ed.), *Das kaiserliche Deutschland*, 119–42.

The formation of the Bordeaux regime has been studied by Frank Herbert Brabant, *The Beginnings of the Third Republic in France: A History of the National Assembly (February-September 1871)* (London, 1940); R. A. Winnacker, "The French Election of 1871," *Papers of the Michigan Academy of Science, Arts, and Letters*, XXII (1936), 477–83; and Robert R. Locke, "A New Look at Conservative Preparations for the French Elections of 1871," *French Historical Studies*, V (1968), 351–58. There is no satisfactory biography of Thiers. The most detailed, based on his personal papers, is by Henri Malo, *Thiers, 1797–1877* (Paris, 1932). Two later attempts, both favorable to him, are Charles Pomaret, *Monsieur Thiers et son siècle* (Paris, 1948), and Georges Roux, *Thiers* (Paris, 1948). Gambetta has fared somewhat better in the hands of J. P. T. Bury, *Gambetta and the National Defence* (New York, 1936); Georges Wormser, *Gambetta dans les tempêtes* (Paris, 1964); and Jacques Chastenet, *Gambetta* (Paris, 1968). The best single statement on the intellectual impact of the war in France is by Claude Digeon, *La crise allemande de la pensée française (1870–1914)* (Paris, 1959). Also see Rudolf Buchner, "Die geistige Reaktion Frankreichs auf die Niederlage von 1871," *Historische Zeitschrift*, CXCV (1962), 614–21; Allan Mitchell, "German History in France after 1870," *Journal of Contemporary History*, 11 (1967), 81–100; and the rather erratic reflections of K. W. Swart, *The Sense of Decadence in Nineteenth-Century France* (The Hague, 1964). An impressionistic comparative essay more concerned with the social setting of the time, especially the plight of the urban poor, is by Pierre-Paul Sagave, *1871. Berlin–Paris: Reichshauptstadt und Hauptstadt der Welt* (Frankfurt, Berlin, Vienna, 1971).

A life's work is recorded in Georges Bourgin, *La guerre de 1870–1871 et la commune* (Paris, 1939) and summarized by him in *La commune*, 3rd ed. (Paris, 1965). Of two older books in English, one tends to be hostile to the subject—Edward S. Mason, *The Paris Commune* (New York, 1930)—and the other highly favorable— Frank Jellinek, *The Paris Commune of 1871* (London, 1937). Brief but incisive is John Plamenatz, *Revolutionary Movement in France, 1815–1871* (London, 1952). Thiers is taken to task by John Roberts, "The Myth of the Commune, 1871," *History Today*, VII (1957), 290–300. Marx's own contribution to the mythology of the Commune is examined by Bertram D. Wolfe, *Marxism. One Hundred Years in the Life of a Doctrine* (New York, 1965). On the fate of the communards see the Marxist work of Jean Bruhat et al., *La commune de 1871* (Paris, 1960), and the two documentary studies, the preface of a major book to come, by Jacques Rougerie, *Procès des communards* (Paris, 1964) and *Paris libre 1871* (Paris, 1971). Especially useful for its review of the bibliography is Roger L. Williams, *The French Revolution of 1870– 1871* (New York, 1969).

Historical literature on French politics after the Commune is extensive. The twin volumes of Daniel Halévy, *La fin des notables* (Paris, 1930), and *La république des ducs* (Paris, 1937), are classics. Perhaps the most reliable guide is still Gabriel Hanotaux, *Histoire de la France contemporaine (1871–1900)*, 4 vols. (Paris, 1903– 1908). More recent attempts tend to be personal commentaries: D. W. Brogan, *The Development of Modern France, 1870–1939* (London, 1940; New York, 1966); Jacques Chastenet, *Histoire de la troisième république,* 7 vols. (Paris, 1952–1963); and Guy Chapman, *The Third Republic of France: The First Phase, 1871–1894* (London, 1962). A clever schematic introduction for the period up to 1879 (another volume is yet to appear) is provided by René Rémond, *La vie politique en France depuis 1789,* 2 vols. (Paris, 1965–1969). On the development of political institutions, see Jacques Gouault, *Comment la France est devenue républicaine, les élections générales et partielles à l'Assemblée nationale (1870–1875)* (Paris, 1954), and François Goguel, *La politique des partis sous la troisième république* (Paris, 1957). The most useful survey in English is David Thomson, *Democracy in France since 1870,* 5th ed. (London, Oxford, New York, 1969). The two best studies of French conservatism are Samuel Osgood, *French Royalism under the Third and Fourth Republics* (The Hague, 1960), and René Rémond, *La droite en France de 1815 à nos jours,* 2nd ed. (Paris, 1963), which is also in English translation (Philadelphia, 1966). To these can be added the recent monographs by Bert Böhmer, *Frankreich zwischen Republik und Monarchie in der Bismarckzeit. Bismarcks Antilegitimismus in französischer Sicht (1870–1877)* (Kallmünz, 1966); Marvin L. Brown, Jr., *The Comte de Chambord: The Third Republic's Uncompromising King* (Durham, N.C., 1967); and, especially competent, John Rothney, *Bonapartism after Sedan* (Ithaca, 1969). Some of the anterior reasons for the presidential crisis in May 1873 are clarified by Robert Schnerb, "La politique fiscale de Thiers," *Revue historique,* CCI (1949), 186–212 and CCII (1949), 184–220, and by Allan Mitchell, "Thiers,

MacMahon, and the Conseil Supérieur de la Guerre,"
French Historical Studies, VI (1969), 232–52. The po-
litical trials of Thiers' successor are related by Jacques
Silvestre de Sacy, *Le maréchal de MacMahon, duc de
Magenta (1808–1893)* (Paris, 1960), and Fresnette
Pisani-Ferry, *Le coup d'état manqué du 16 mai 1877*
(Paris, 1965); both draw on MacMahon's unpublished
memoirs.

The diplomatic history of the period after 1870 is
best told in the peerless volume of William L. Langer,
European Alliances and Alignments, 1871–1890, 2nd ed.
(New York, 1964). One can also turn to the well-tem-
pered survey by Pierre Renouvin et al., *Histoire des relations internationales*, 8 vols. (Paris, 1953–1958), and the
arresting, less cautious views of A. J. P. Taylor, *The
Struggle for Mastery in Europe, 1848–1918* (Oxford,
1954). Despite their age and brevity, G. P. Gooch,
Franco-German Relations, 1871–1914 (London, 1923),
and Georg Rosen, *Die Stellungnahme der Politik Bismarcks zur Frage der Staatsform in Frankreich von 1871–
1890* (Detmold, 1924), are still serviceable commentaries.
Norman Rich, *Friedrich von Holstein. Politics and
Diplomacy in the Era of Bismarck and Wilhelm II*, 2 vols.
(Cambridge, 1965), and George O. Kent, *Arnim and Bismarck* (Oxford, 1968), have both made competent
evaluations of German statesmen at odds with Bismarck's
foreign policy. His financial connections form the theme
of a forthcoming study announced in an essay by Fritz
Stern, "Gold and Iron: the Collaboration and Friendship
of Gerson Bleichröder and Otto von Bismarck," *American Historical Review*, LXXV (1969), 37–46. On the
most controversial international incident of the period,
consult Hans Herzfeld, *Die deutsch-französische Kriegs-*

gefahr von 1875 (Berlin, 1922), and the critical reassessment by Andreas Hillgruber, "Die 'Krieg-in-Sicht'-Krise–Wegscheide der Politik der europäischen Grossmächte in der späten Bismarck-Zeit," in Ernst Schulin (ed.), *Gedenkschrift Martin Göhring. Studien zur europäischen Geschichte* (Wiesbaden, 1968), 239–53. Curiously, there is no worthwhile monograph on the subject in French. Concerning the sequel, four older works are all solid but suffer from a foreshortening of perspective: Robert H. Wienefeld, *Franco-German Relations, 1878–1885* (Baltimore, 1929); Pearl Boring Mitchell, *The Bismarckian Policy of Conciliation with France, 1875–1885* (Philadelphia, 1935); W. N. Medlicott, *The Congress of Berlin and After: A Diplomatic History of the Near Eastern Settlement, 1878–1880* (London, 1938); and Wolfgang Windelband, *Bismarck und die europäischen Grossmächte 1879–1885* (Essen, 1940). The role of the press has been researched with incredible diligence by E. Malcolm Carroll in *French Public Opinion and Foreign Affairs, 1870–1914* (New York and London, 1931), and in *Germany and the Great Powers, 1866–1914. A Study in Public Opinion and Foreign Policy* (New York, 1938).

Much more in the forefront of discussion at present are the commercial, industrial, and technological developments in the latter part of the nineteenth century. A pioneering work was the monograph of Ivo Nikolai Lambi, *Free Trade and Protection in Germany, 1868–1879* (Wiesbaden, 1963), which preceded the broader and less disciplined work of Helmut Böhme already cited. Theoretically more challenging than either, treating the "trend period" from 1873 to 1896, is the provocative essay of Hans Rosenberg, *Grosse Depression und Bismarckzeit. Wirtschaft, Gesellschaft und Politik in Mittel-*

europa (Berlin, 1967). For the other side of the Rhine, see
Rondo E. Cameron, *France and the Economic Develop-
ment of Europe, 1800–1914* (Princeton, 1961), and
Charles P. Kindleberger, *Economic Growth in France
and Britain, 1851–1950* (Cambridge, Mass., 1964). Of
particular interest is the article by Cameron, "Economic
Growth and Stagnation in France, 1815–1914," *Journal
of Modern History*, XXX (1958), 1–13, which ascribes
France's relatively disappointing performance after 1870
to a deficiency of demand and higher costs of production.
Dated but still useful as a reference is J. H. Clapham, *The
Economic Development of France and Germany, 1815–
1914*, 4th ed. (Cambridge, 1966). The statistical comparison of Paul Bairoch, "Niveaux de développement
économique de 1810 à 1910," *Annales*, XX (1965), 1091–
1117, is to be used with caution. Such is not the case for the
authoritative survey by David S. Landes, *The Unbound
Prometheus. Technological Change and Industrial Development in Western Europe from 1750 to the Present*
(Cambridge, 1969). A clear presentation which rounds
out the century is by Raymond Poidevin, *Les relations
économiques et financières entre la France et l'Allemagne
de 1898 à 1914* (Paris, 1969).

Closely related is the subject of an earlier synthesis
by Maurice Baumont, *L'essor industriel et l'impérialisme
colonial (1878–1904)* (Paris, 1937). To be recommended
as an introduction to the vast literature on the building of
the French empire is the disabused commentary of Henri
Brunschwig, *Mythes et réalités de l'impérialisme colonial
français, 1871–1914* (Paris, 1960), available in English
translation (London, 1966). For Germany one might consult A. J. P. Taylor, *Germany's First Bid for Colonies,
1884–1885* (New York, 1938), who takes the traditional

view that Bismarck intended to distract French interest from European affairs. But the dominating work in this area is now that of Hans-Ulrich Wehler, *Bismarck und der Imperialismus* (Cologne and Berlin, 1969), who sees the chancellor's "pragmatic expansionism" as symptomatic of his unresolved domestic problems and charges him with resorting to "Bonapartist" expediencies. A thesis similar to Wehler's is stated in a much narrower context by Hartmut Pogge von Strandmann, "Domestic Origins of Germany's Colonial Expansion under Bismarck," *Past and Present*, No. 42 (1969), 140–59. The formation and influence of pressure groups in imperial Germany is a topic which is only beginning to receive the attention it deserves. Compare Gerhard Schulz, "Über Entstehung und Formen von Interessengruppen in Deutschland seit Beginn der Industrialisierung," and Thomas Nipperdey, "Interessenverbände und Parteien in Deutschland vor dem Ersten Weltkrieg," *Politische Vierteljahresschrift*, II (1961), 124–54, 262–80. Also see the monographs by Hans-Jürgen Puhle, *Agrarische Interessenpolitik und preussischer Konservatismus im wilhelminischen Reich 1893–1914* (Hanover, 1966), and Hartmut Kaelble, *Industrielle Interessenpolitik in der wilhelminischen Gesellschaft* (Berlin, 1967). Commenting on these, Helmut Böhme, "Politik und Ökonomie in der Reichsgründungs- und späten Bismarckzeit," in Stürmer (ed.), *Das kaiserliche Deutschland*, 26–50, concludes that Bismarck's "Sammlungspolitik" after 1878 concealed but could not obviate the fundamental conflict between agrarian and industrial interests. These new studies owe much to the belated influence of Eckart Kehr, whose scattered essays have been collected posthumously as *Der Primat der Innenpolitik. Gesammelte Aufsätze zur preussisch-*

deutschen Sozialgeschichte im 19. und 20. Jahrhundert (Berlin, 1965). For more general descriptions of the development of German social patterns, see Ralf Dahrendorf, *Gesellschaft und Demokratie in Deutschland* (Munich, 1965), translated by the author (New York, 1967), and Karl Erich Born, "Der soziale und wirtschaftliche Strukturwandel Deutschlands am Ende des 19. Jahrhunderts," *Vierteljahrsschrift für Sozial- und Wirtschaftsgeschichte*, L (1963), 361–76. On France one may select the earlier work of Charles Morazé, *La France bourgeoise* (Paris, 1946), and the broad survey of the years from 1840 to 1914 by Pierre Sorlin, *La société française* (Paris, 1969).

It must suffice here to suggest only a few representative titles dealing with the socialist movements in Germany and France before 1890. The most interesting recent books on the former are by Guenther Roth, *The Social Democrats in Imperial Germany. A Study in Working-Class Isolation and National Integration* (Totowa, N.J., 1963); Vernon L. Lidtke, *The Outlawed Party. Social Democracy in Germany, 1878–1890* (Princeton, 1966); and Hans-Ulrich Wehler, *Sozialdemokratie und Nationalstaat*, 2nd ed. (Würzburg, 1971). The reorganization of the French labor movement has been investigated by Jean T. Joughin, *The Paris Commune in French Politics, 1871–1880*, 2 vols. (Baltimore, 1955); Aaron Noland, *The Founding of the French Socialist Party* (Cambridge, Mass., 1956); and Daniel Ligou, *Histoire du socialisme en France, 1871–1961* (Paris, 1961). A comparison of the two traditions has been suggested by Milorad M. Drachkovitch, *Les socialismes français et allemand et le problème de la guerre* (Geneva, 1953).

A comparative study of anticlericalism in Germany and France needs to be written. A barely adequate basis is afforded by Georg Franz, *Kulturkampf: Staat und katholische Kirche in Mitteleuropa von der Säkularisation bis zum Abschluss des preussischen Kulturkampfes* (Munich, 1954), and by Erich Schmidt-Volkmar, *Der Kulturkampf in Deutschland 1871–1890* (Göttingen, 1962). New information is now being made available through the opening of the Vatican archives for this period, as evidenced by the first volume of Rudolf Lill (ed.), *Vatikanische Akten zur Geschichte des deutschen Kulturkampfes* (Tübingen, 1970). Also employing newly accessible Vatican resources, as well as material gathered from Church archives throughout France, is the splendid work of Jacques Gadille, *La pensée et l'action politiques des évêques français au début de la IIIe république 1870/1883*, 2 vols. (Paris, 1967). Otherwise we are still dependent on monographs such as Evelyn Acomb, *The French Laic Laws, 1879–1889. The First Anti-Clerical Campaign of the Third French Republic* (New York, 1941); or on the sweeping surveys of Adrien Dansette, *Histoire religieuse de la France contemporaine*, 2 vols. (Paris, 1948–1951), and André Latreille et al., *Histoire du catholicisme en France*, 3 vols. (Paris, 1957–1962).

The history of Germany's military establishment has been most searchingly illuminated by two scholars whose work has been previously mentioned, Gerhard Ritter and Gordon A. Craig. To these should be added the standard account of Karl Demeter, *Das deutsche Offizierkorps in Gesellschaft und Staat 1650–1945*, 4th ed. (Frankfurt, 1965). The latest commentary, which indicates the current state of research, is by Manfred Messerschmidt, "Die Armee in Staat und Gesellschaft—

Die Bismarckzeit," in Stürmer (ed.), *Das kaiserliche Deutschland*, 89–118. Comparable to Demeter is the original work of Raoul Girardet, *La société militaire dans la France contemporaine, 1815–1939* (Paris, 1953). In addition, French military reforms and preparations after 1870 are the subject of a number of excellent studies. The most recent are Richard D. Challener, *The French Theory of the Nation in Arms, 1866–1939* (New York, 1955); Henry Contamine, *La revanche, 1871–1914* (Paris, 1957); Eugène Carrias, *La pensée militaire française* (Paris, 1960); Paul-Marie de la Gorce, *La république et son armée* (Paris, 1963); and David B. Ralston, *The Army of the Republic. The Place of the Military in the Political Evolution of France, 1871–1914* (Cambridge, Mass., and London, 1967). The possibility of a more comparative approach is exemplified by Corelli Barnett, "The Education of Military Elites," *Journal of Contemporary History*, II (1967), 15–35.

For the year 1887 and following it is worthwhile to consult the summary chapter entitled "Der konservative Ausgang der Bismarckzeit" which concludes the fundamental volume of Heinrich Heffter, *Die deutsche Selbstverwaltung im 19. Jahrhundert* (Stuttgart, 1950); Heffter chastises Bismarck's "dictatorial will to power" and contrasts this to the emergence of liberal democracy in France. But that France was not without problems of its own, even before the Dreyfus affair, is clear from Adrien Dansette, *Le boulangisme*, 16th ed. (Paris, 1946). Little is added by Fresnette Pisani-Ferry, *Le général Boulanger* (Paris, 1969), who also assumes the biographical and transitory nature of Boulangism. Yet its broader significance in the evolution of the French parliamentary system is pointed out by Frederic H. Seager, *The*

Boulanger Affair. Political Crossroad of France, 1886–1889 (Ithaca, 1969). The transformation of militant French nationalism from a jacobin to a reactionary cause is sketched by Jacques Droz, "Der Nationalismus der Linken und der Nationalismus der Rechten in Frankreich (1871–1914)," *Historische Zeitschrift*, CCX (1970), 1–13. The controversy surrounding Bismarck's final diplomatic achievements has been collected by Hans Hallmann (ed.), *Zur Geschichte und Problematik des deutsch-russischen Rückversicherungsvertrages von 1887* (Darmstadt, 1968). This should be augmented by the essay of Hans-Ulrich Wehler, "Bismarcks Imperialismus und späte Russlandpolitik unter dem Primat der Innenpolitik," in Stürmer (ed.), *Das kaiserliche Deutschland*, 235–64, which places blame above all on Bismarck's shortsighted economic policy for the eventual formation of a Paris-Petersburg entente. As an investigation of that subject, the craftsmanship of William L. Langer, *The Franco-Russian Alliance, 1890–1894* (Cambridge, Mass., 1929), is still admirable, the date of publication and the methodological objections of some younger historians notwithstanding. The circumstances and consequences of William II's accession and Bismarck's dismissal have been often related, seldom more readably than by Michael Balfour, *The Kaiser and His Times* (London, 1964). The latest scholarly analysis, which compares Bismarck's deliberate intimidation of France in the early 1870's with the threat after 1878 to overturn Germany's entire constitutional system, is by Michael Stürmer, "Staatsstreichgedanken im Bismarckreich," *Historische Zeitschrift*, CCIX (1969), 556–615. The eventual French reaction to Germany's Weltpolitik after 1890 is best described by Eugen Weber, *The Nationalist Revival in France, 1905–1914*

(Berkeley, 1959), and by Gilbert Ziebura, *Die deutsche Frage in der öffentlichen Meinung Frankreichs von 1911–1914* (Berlin-Dahlem, 1955).

Anyone who wants to search more widely, particularly into literary topics, might begin by consulting *Deutschland-Frankreich. Ludwigsburger Beiträge zum Problem der deutsch-französischen Beziehungen*, 4 vols. (Stuttgart, 1954–1966).

NOTES

Following are the abbreviations used to indicate the major published documentary collections which are most frequently cited. The documents are identified by number, rather than pagination, except when otherwise noted.

APP Historische Reichskommission. *Die auswärtige Politik Preussens 1858–1871.* 10 vols., Berlin, 1932–1939.

DDF Ministère des affaires étrangères. *Documents diplomatiques français (1871–1914)*, 1re série (1871–1900). 15 vols., Paris, 1929–1959.

GP Johannes Lepsius, Albrecht Mendelssohn-Bartholdy, and Friedrich Thimme. *Die Grosse Politik der europäischen Kabinette 1871–1914.* 40 vols., Berlin, 1922–1927.

GW Herman von Petersdorf et al. *Bismarck. Die gesammelten Werke.* 15 vols., Berlin, 1924–1935.

OD Ministère des affaires étrangères. *Les origines diplomatiques de la guerre de 1870/71. Receuil de documents officiels.* 29 vols., Paris, 1910–1932.

I

1. Quoted by Erich Marcks, *Bismarcks Jugend 1815–1848* (Stuttgart and Berlin, 1909), 108. The dating of this remark, mistakenly given here as 1844, is corrected by Marcks himself on page 167.
2. Otto von Bismarck, *Gedanken und Erinnerungen*, 3 vols. (Stuttgart and Berlin, 1922), I, 1–3.
3. Marcks, *op. cit.*, 449–51.
4. GW I, 75, 76.

5. GW I, 272, 291, 298.
6. GW I, 312.
7. GW I, 562; GW II, 45.
8. GW II, 91. Robert von Keudell, *Fürst und Fürstin Bismarck* (Berlin and Stuttgart, 1901), 51.
9. GW II, 152.
10. *Ibid.*
11. GW II, 236, 237, 245, 246. Keudell, *op. cit.*, 56. The view that it may be taken as "certain" that Napoleon expressed the wish for a Prussian alliance is held by Herbert Geuss, *Bismarck und Napoleon III.* (Cologne and Graz, 1959), 48. The evidence, however, does not permit such certainty.
12. GW II, 253.
13. GW XIV, 686.
14. GW III, 27.
15. GW III, 44.
16. GW III, 59.
17. GW III, 127.
18. GW III, 176.
19. GW III, 326.
20. GW III, 354, 355.

II

1. GW II, 253.
2. For the details, see Helmut Böhme, *Deutschlands Weg zur Grossmacht* (Cologne and Berlin, 1966), 100–20.
3. GW IV, 433, 477, 478; GW V, 37.
4. GW IV, 6.
5. GW IV, 42, 82, 149, 150, 190–2. APP IV, 581. For a convenient summary of Franco-Prussian diplomatic relations during the Polish and Schleswig-Holstein controversies, see Geuss, *Bismarck und Napoleon III.*, 77–112.
6. GW IV, 334, 344, 364, 369, 458.
7. GW IV, 440, 442.

8. GW V, 51, 54, 61, 99, 163.

9. GW V, 163, 164. APP VI, 100,

10. OD VI, 1528. GW V, 165, 172, 173, 180, 184. Hermann Oncken, *Die Rheinpolitik des Kaisers Napoleon III.*, 3 vols. (Stuttgart, Berlin, Leipzig), I, 65–9 (No. 24). Keudell, *Fürst und Fürstin Bismarck*, 225–7.

11. GW V, 188–90, 196, 197, 205; GW XIV, 1129. This version is corroborated by Napoleon's own testimony that Bismarck "did not make me any formal proposition. For my part, I did not express to him any personal desire whatsoever." Emile Ollivier, *L'empire libéral*, 18 vols. (Paris, 1895–1918), VII, 475.

12. This remark was made by Count Esterházy at a cabinet meeting on February 21. Heinrich Ritter von Srbik (ed.), *Quellen zur deutschen Politik Österreichs, 1859–1866*, 5 vols. (Oldenburg, 1934–1938), V, 2325.

13. GW V, 250. APP VI, 499.

14. GW V, 251.

15. Oncken, *op. cit.*, I, 145–50 (No. 75).

III

1. Oncken, *Rheinpolitik*, I, 98–9 (No. 38). GW VI, 453.

2. Bismarck, *Gedanken und Erinnerungen*, II, 36–55.

3. GW VI, 460.

4. GW VI, 480.

5. GW VI, 497.

6. GW VI, 521, 530, 531.

7. GW VI, 579.

8. Böhme, *Deutschlands Weg zur Grossmacht*, 213–66.

9. GW VI, 606.

10. Hajo Holborn (ed.), *Aufzeichnungen und Erinnerungen aus dem Leben des Botschafters Joseph Marie von Radowitz*, 2 vols. (Berlin and Leipzig, 1925), I, 124–32. GW VI, 623, 642, 648.

11. GW VIa, 899, 917.

12. GW VI, 625, 637.
13. GW VI, 643, 667, 675.
14. GW VI, 683, 684, 708.
15. GW VI, 719, 728, 733, 750. APP VIII, 398.
16. GW VI, 764, 816, 823.
17. GW VIa, 825, 828.
18. GW VIa, 853.
19. GW X, pp. 464–5.
20. Oncken, *op. cit.*, III, 185–8 (No. 698), 268 (No. 753).
21. GW VIa, 1127, 1146, 1154.
22. GW VIa, 1218, 1323; GW VIb, 1327.
23. GW VIb, 1389.
24. GW VIb, 1403, 1405, 1449. OD XXVI, 7970. Keudell, *Fürst und Fürstin Bismarck*, 419–20.
25. GW VIb, 1557.
26. Oncken, *op. cit.*, III, 396–7 (No. 845). GW VIb, 1573, 1588.
27. GW VIb, 1591.
28. GW VIb, 1597, 1598, 1602, 1611.

IV

1. GW VIb, 1747. Moritz Busch, *Graf Bismarck und seine Leute während des Krieges mit Frankreich*, 7th ed. (Leipzig, 1889), 23–4. Heinrich von Poschinger, *Fürst Bismarck, Neue Tischgespräche und Interviews*, 2 vols. (Stuttgart and Leipzig, 1899), II, 48.
2. GW VIb, 1755, 1782.
3. GW VIb, 1736.
4. GW VIb, 1755. Busch, *op. cit.*, 39–40.
5. GW VIb, 1761.
6. *Bismarcks Briefe an seine Gattin aus dem Kriege 1870/71* (Stuttgart and Berlin, 1903), 36.
7. GW VIb, 1773, 1774.
8. *Bismarcks Briefe an seine Gattin*, 39.

9. Jules Favre, *Gouvernement de la défense nationale*, 3 vols. (Paris, 1871–1875), I, 383–6.

10. *Bismarcks Briefe an seine Gattin*, 40. GW VIb, 1788, 1789.

11. GW VIb, 1812.

12. GW VIb, 1817, 1824, 1826, 1835. Favre, *op. cit.*, I, 153–206.

13. GW VIb, 1764.

14. Adolphe Thiers, *Notes et souvenirs, 1870–1873* (Paris, 1903), 3–57.

15. GW VIb, 1801, 1806.

16. GW VIb, 1808. *Bismarcks Briefe an seine Gattin*, 43.

17. GW VIb, 1824, 1839, 1848, 1858, 1859, 1869.

18. *Bismarcks Briefe an seine Gattin*, 54. GW II, 1382; GW VIb, 1885.

19. Bismarck, *Gedanken und Erinnerungen*, II, 107–33.

20. GW VIb, 1900, 1903, 1907–9, 1911. Thiers, *op. cit.*, 61–106. Favre, *op cit.*, II, 1–87. Busch, *op. cit.* 244–62, 271–6.

21. GW II, 1369, 1374, 1378, 1383, 1405; GW VIb, 1951, 1952, 1956, 1976, 1989, 2002, 2005.

22. *Bismarcks Briefe an seine Gattin*, 60.

23. GW VIb, 2012.

24. GW VIb, 2014, 2016. Favre, *op. cit.*, II, 362–417.

25. GW VIb, 2010, 2014. The final text of the armistice agreement is printed in Favre, *op. cit.*, II, 493–9.

26. Charles de Rémusat, *Mémoires de ma vie*, 5 vols. (Paris, 1958–1967), V, 359. This phase is ascribed to the Vicomte de Meaux by Henri Malo, *Thiers, 1797–1877* (Paris, 1932), 487–8. In *Souvenirs Politiques, 1871–1877* (Paris, 1905), 19, Meaux elaborates: "Ce qui rendait M. Thiers inévitable et lui valait de paraître l'élu de la nation même, c'était son opposition depuis quinze ans à tout ce qui avait préparé ou venait de consommer la ruine de la France."

27. Favre, *op. cit.*, III, 71–6.

28. *Bismarcks Briefe an seine Gattin*, 86. Thiers, *op. cit.*, pp. 109–27. Favre, *op. cit.*, III, 89–120.

V

1. For a typical example of Bismarck's use of the term *bündnisfähig* after 1870, see GP I, 151.
2. GP I, 1. DDF I, 1.
3. GP I, 12. Favre, *Gouvernement*, III, 163–8.
4. GP I, 2–4, 7–9. Favre, *op. cit.*, III, 227–334. Thiers, *Notes et souvenirs*, 141–70.
5. GP I, 5, 8.
6. GP I, 11, 14–7. DDF I, 2–4. Favre, *op. cit.*, III, 335–76. An English translation of the definitive settlement can be found in Robert I. Giesberg, *The Treaty of Frankfort* (Philadelpha, 1966), 283–93.
7. GP I, 19.
8. GP I, 35, 38, 59.
9. GP I, 23, 30, 36–9, 54, 60. DDF I, 80, 101. GW II, 1482.
10. GP I, 69, 71, 90, 91.
11. *Ibid.*
12. GP I, 66.
13. GP I, 93, 95.
14. GP I, 92.
15. GW VIc, 7. GP I, 120–30.
16. GP I, 114, 115. GW II, 1491; GW VIc, 43. DDF I, 206, 208, 209, 213–5. Bismarck, *Gedanken und Erinnerungen*, II, 186–93. Vicomte de Gontaut-Biron, *Mon ambassade en Allemagne (1872–1873)* (Paris, 1906), 346–73.
17. GP I, 131–50. DDF I, 244, 248, 251, 253, 257, 259, 263, 266–9, 273, 281. André Dreux, *Dernières années de l'ambassade en Allemagne de M. de Gontaut-Biron, 1874–1877* (Paris, 1907), 1–35.
18. GP I, 151.
19. GP I, 155–93. GW VIc, 72. DDF I, 358–440.

20. GP I, 210–14. GW II, 1579. DDF II, 166, 167, 172, 198, 209, 212, 222, 250. *Denkwürdigkeiten des Fürsten Chlodwig zu Hohenlohe-Schillingsfürst*, 2 vols. (Stuttgart and Leipzig, 1907), II, 215–26.

VI

1. GP II, 416. DDF II, 219, 267, 273, 316, 317, 319, 320, 322–4, 327.
2. GP III, 658. Auguste Scheurer-Kestner, *Souvenirs de jeunesse* (Paris, 1905), 262–3.
3. GW VIII, 202.
4. GW II, 1623.
5. GP III, 656, 661, 662, 668–70, 672. DDF II, 369, 390, 440, 467.
6. GP III, 677, 680, 681, 684–99. DDF V, 249, 264, 385, 395, 406, 450–3, 455–61, 467, 468.
7. GP III, 676.
8. GW VIc, 299. GP III, 683, 702; GP VI, 1269.
9. GP III, 707. Norman Rich and M. H. Fisher (eds.), *The Holstein Papers*, 4 vols. (Cambridge, 1955–1963), II, 160–2, 200–1.
10. Ivo Nikolai Lambi, *Free Trade and Protection in Germany, 1868–1879* (Wiesbaden, 1963), 226–40.
11. GP I, 193. GW II, 1564; GW VIc, 346.
12. Henri Rochefort, *Les aventures de ma vie*, 5 vols. (Paris, n.d.), V, 3. Freycinet admits that Boulanger was chosen to give some radical republican balance to an otherwise moderate regime but neglects to mention Clémenceau's part in the decision. Charles de Freycinet, *Souvenirs, 1878–1893*, 6th ed. (Paris, 1914), 328–33.
13. GP VI, 1227. Walter Bussmann (ed.), *Staatssekretär Graf Herbert von Bismarck. Aus seiner politischen Privatkorrespondenz* (Göttingen, 1964), 424–5 (No. 282).
14. GP VI, 1200, 1203–6, 1228–30, 1238, 1239.

15. GP VI, 1236, 1237.
16. GP VI, 1240, 1241.
17. *Ibid.* Horst Kohl (ed.), *Die politischen Reden des Fürsten Bismarck*, 14 vols. (Stuttgart, 1892–1905), XII, 175–204.
18. GP VI, 1242, 1244, 1249. DDF VI, 419.
19. GP VI, 1213.
20. GP VI, 1257–64, 1272, 1273. DDF VI, 498–524.
21. GP V, 1068, 1070, 1076–92; GP VI, 1214, 1215. DDF VI, 562.
22. GP VI, 1340, 1341. Bismarck, *Gedanken und Erinnerungen*, III, 121–46.

INDEX